The Trinity College VIII

About the Author

David Hickey, born and educated in Ireland, has since worked mostly in the financial arena. When not falling out of a sculling boat, he continues to work on a non-executive basis in various companies. He lives in London with his wife, Jane, and two mad cocker spaniels. They have three grown-up children.

The Trinity College VIII

Rowing for the Ladies Plate

David Hickey

The Liffey Press

Published by
The Liffey Press Ltd
'Clareville'
307 Clontarf Road
Dublin D03 PO46, Ireland
www.theliffeypress.com

A catalogue record of this book is
available from the British Library.

ISBN 978-1-8383593-6-2

Printed by W&G Baird in Antrim.

CONTENTS

TROUBLE STARTS

YEAR ZERO

YEAR ONE

YEAR TWO

YEAR FINAL

Please don't lend this book to anyone. Instead, tell everyone you know to buy their own copy. The royalties from any sales resulting will be donated to organisations that support the sport of rowing.

The film rights, however, have been reserved by the author to ensure that Tom Cruise doesn't get to play him in the inevitable Hollywood blockbuster.

This book is dedicated to Jane, and Alexander, Sally, and Jess, and to the late Tom, Brian, Noel, the late Robin, Nick, the late Rob, Chris, Donagh, Jarlath, John, Rory, David, James, David and Jane, Ted, Richard and Kieran. I guess you know your own surnames …

I am grateful especially to my wife Jane Hickey (née Johnston) for her rigorous final review, as well as to my sister Toey and friend Ian McMillan for their early editorial comments, and also for their ability to swear blind that they actually enjoyed reading it. I know the truth. I am also particularly grateful to Dave Sanfey for supplying many of the photographs in this book.

There are no mistakes within these pages, but if there were, they would all be the fault of someone else.

TROUBLE STARTS

A General Invitation

'Is that Dublin University Boat Club?' the Gruff Voice asked.

I had picked up the black Bakelite telephone on the second ring, glancing around the Boat Club rooms as I did so. Three of the lads were squashed onto the tired old sofa, snoozing, grunting and farting, often all three, and three more members were lounging around the window on the ground floor of the oldest building in Trinity College, discussing the talent walking past.

The building is known as the Rubrics, possibly because every female undergraduate who entered it has rued the day, or more likely the night, or perhaps it is because the bricks in the walls are red. I lean towards the former as the more likely explanation since that would also explain the bricks being red through embarrassment. Those were randy days back in the 1700s when the building was designed and erected, or built, if you prefer. Not like the 1970s. None of that naughty stuff went on when I was at the university. Or so the governing authorities said, so it must have been true.

The Rubrics, oldest building in Trinity College

Anyway, back to the telephone.

'Yes, this is DUBC,' I said.

'Well then,' said the Gruff Voice. 'This is General Fayez Yakan, President of the Egyptian Rowing Federation and you are hereby invited to the Festival of the Nile on the nineteenth of December in Cairo. Will you attend?'

I turned around fully into the room, totally confused, having only half listened. Clearly I had paid him about as much attention as I did to my unfortunate lecturers.

'Who is it, Dave?' asked Rory.

Having only to read picture comics for his Geology degree, Rory had oodles of time to sit in the Boat Club rooms and oversee the day's intellectual and philosophical discussions. As if. Also, being much older, he used to keep an eye out for my welfare. Lord knows I needed someone to protect me from myself.

Anyway, back (again) to the call. Holding the phone down low I said, 'Some fellow who says he's a General and would we row in Cairo,' I replied neutrally, trying desperately not to look uncool as I said the ludicrous words.

The lads by the window turned round and the grins and banter started. 'Sure it wasn't Khartoum, Dave?'

'Or was it Cartoon?' How they laughed. Smart arse comedians.

Rory looked at me in a resigned sort of way.

'Dave, I keep telling you, there are so many nutters around, he's just the first today.'

'Sure,' I said, 'but what should I do?'

'Tell him to feck off and keep taking the pills.'

'Oh, okay.'

I put the phone back to my mouth.

'Did you get that? Feck off and keep taking the pills.'

I slammed the phone down in the most masculine fashion that I could muster (squashing my knuckles horribly on the phone cradle as I did so) and tried desperately to tune back into the debate about the merits or otherwise of one of the girls passing outside the window.

I didn't really know much about girls. I have two sisters, Carolyn, the calm and diplomatic one, and Joyce, the even calmer and more diplomatic one, but they're not 'girls' if you're their brother, if you know what I mean. My problem was that I had always attended single sex schools, and for my final four years I was a boarder in one run by priests. They didn't seem to know much about girls either. Mind you, a few of them knew about boys, but that was a long time ago and the rules were different then, as their defence counsels might have argued.

But most of all, rowing was the wrong sport to embrace if you wanted to meet girls. The first problem was that oarsmen can't drink as it is usually banned by their fascist coaches, outside the very rare training breaks. That meant there was little point in going down to the pub with the rest of one's class sitting there nursing a coke all evening. I mean, isn't alcohol the whole point of attending university? So you were immediately marked down as some sort of boring freak.

Then came the training problem. Everyone knew it was severe and so they deduced you had to be some sort of sadist or masochist, likely both, and hence definitely to be avoided. It also meant that you were out of sight for most of the day, and even when you were in evidence at lectures or seminars, you were normally asleep with exhaustion. So no chance of chatting up girls there either.

But it got even worse than that at Trinity. There, rowing seemed to be an invisible sport. The rugby buggers after all had their playing pitch right in the middle of the campus. And since a few of them in those amateur days were on the Irish squad at the same time, they tended to trot around college like prize bulls dispensing, well I don't quite know what, but I could make a squeamish guess.

And the fair weather cricketers and half fit soccer fellows had their creases and pitches also plumb in the university centre. So they could also strut around like prize peacocks eyeing up the girls when they should have been watching their balls, as it were. Mind you, I'm not saying that they didn't do that as well. Some of them did look somewhat cross eyed to my cynical peepers.

Rowers, on the other hand, were invisible. We did weightlifting in a filthy boiler room hidden around the back of the college buildings. We went running in the dark. And when we clambered into boats it was in far off Islandbridge, about as remote from the campus as the middle of the bog, at least to smooth young South Dublin girls on the lookout for a handsome catch.

We rowers had no chance. So looking, drooling, and dreaming was all we could do. Hence the gang at the window acting like monkeys in the zoo, only in this case the ogling was being done by the primates on the inside of the glass, and not the innocents walking past outside.

Return of the General

I remember training was tough that day (as it was every bloody day). The University First VIII was slowly coming together. The big target for the year had been set, but competition for places was fierce. That day there was a heavy weights session at lunchtime, followed by an hour's run at 6.00 pm in the evening. Despite having bulked up a few stone over the previous three years, at 6 feet, 3 inches and barely 13 stone, I was still too light and therefore desperate to lift some semi-serious weights. So it was a hard session, and not uncompetitive with the others there at the same time.

Unfortunately, I was not a quick runner either, and so I was worried that I might struggle to stay aboard what was starting to look like a serious boat. So I had to push as hard as I could on the run also. I felt I could deliver a rowing rhythm though and keep time (some said keeping time was all I could do), so I had a chance. Accordingly, I had the biggest supper I could afford to buy and headed for an early bed. After all that punishment, I slept late the next morning.

The phone woke me. I was the resident in the Boat Club rooms that year so stumbled out of the bedroom and across past the long suffering smelly sofa, and grabbed the black lump on its fourth ring.

'Is that Dublin University Boat Club?' came the Gruff Voice again.

I sighed. I'd been woken for this?

'Yes,' I said in a resigned tone and went to hang up.

'Before you put the phone down, young man, I *have* been taking the pills, but I am *still* General Fayez Yakan, President of the Egyptian Rowing Federation, and you are *still* invited to the Festival of the Nile on the nineteenth of December in Cairo.'

Days later, a confirmatory telegram (Google it if you're under sixty – it is in the history section of Wikipedia) duly arrived so it was all starting to look real. Then the first wobble appeared. The club notified the Irish Amateur Rowing Union about the invitation which, understandably, felt that this being a prestigious international event, they needed to be certain that Trinity were the fastest of the domestic university crews. I guess they also wanted to be sure that if Trinity were to travel, the students concerned would take the event seriously. Accordingly, a race was set up. So early morning rowing outings were immediately added to the existing daily training schedule.

It was bitterly cold that November. I recall ice on the sides of the upper reaches of the Liffey where we trained each morning as dawn broke. We started by shivering our way up and down the river practicing starts and sprints. There was a little more pressure pushed my way as I had been moved into the stroke seat. (The stroke man sits in the stern of the boat, opposite the cox, and is principally responsible for setting the rowing rate and rhythm for the crew.) John (our usual stroke man) was doing his usual first term sabbatical and for that reason I was handed the responsibility.

That cold snap did bring clear skies, however, and so once we had warmed up the rowing conditions turned out to be glorious. The water resembled a glass mirror. It was ripple-free and perfectly reflected the emerging blue sky above. There was utter silence in the river surroundings.

As we rowed along, the only sound was the single splash of the eight oars entering the water simultaneously, the grating of the outboard riggers as the oars went through their rowing arcs, and then the slam as each rowing stroke finished, and the eight blades emerged in unison from the crystalline water. Then utter silence again as the crew moved up on their eight seats, positioned over the parallel slides beneath, gathering for the next stroke, followed by the repeat splash as the next cycle commenced.

On and on, silence, splash and slam, silence, splash and slam, one metronomically following the other. They say that golfers will return for another eighteen holes if they make one outstanding shot in a round. Rowing outings, where the world is distilled into a single task, without interruption or distraction, is why oarsmen return. It can get Zen-like.

The extra outings paid off as we duly headed out to the nearest lake at the chosen weekend where the qualifying race was to take place, and luckily we won it comfortably enough.

There was one more obstacle to be overcome however. Injections. We were told we had to be loaded up with a taste of all manner of horrible diseases before we would be let into Egypt. And so on one dark wet afternoon we duly trudged into the college medical rooms to be needled in sequence. The nurse was quite officious.

'Line up in a row, roll up your left sleeves, and look away.'

We did it in crew order, so I was last up.

'Excuse me, I don't wish to seem awkward,' I said, 'but I pass out when people inject me.'

'Nonsense,' said the doctor, 'big fella like you, hold still there.'

I did as I was told, he stabbed me and I fell over. On top of him. He crashed down and hit his head on the corner of the desk. Apparently he bled like something out of a Sam Peckinpah movie. The nurse was furiously crocheting his scalp as the lads scooped me up and hauled me off before he could recover and get to me. I had no idea what had gone on. I came to as I was being carried across Front Square out of his reach. Funnily enough, I was never sick enough subsequently ever to need his services again.

The General in Person

All of this drivel goes to explain why, on the morning of nineteenth of December, 1976, the crew, with rowing coach Nick Tinne, blinked its way into the bright sunshine as we disembarked the EgyptAir flight from London and headed for our designated transport coach.

What a tour. There wasn't much opposition for the racing really. Only some of the finest rowing university crews in the world. The Sorbonne from Paris, with a lady coach and her daughter, who was so utterly gorgeous she silenced every oarsman in every room she entered. I've seen dogs drool less over fresh bones. It was pathetic really, but that's oarsmen for you.

Then there was Oxford, led by the ubiquitous Dan Topolski, whose fame (for rowing mostly) had spread even into Dublin's rowing fraternity. The university of the giants, otherwise known as the Washington Huskies, showed up, and of course the Harvard boys were there, born to rule the world, as they saw it. Not to mention the local crews. The Arab Contractors and the Cairo Police crews were out in force, desperate to take down a few Western scalps.

But back to my General. The Festival Ball on the final official night of the tour was a glamorous affair. Luckily, the DUBC Senior blazer and waistcoat are both black with white piping, so all we needed to look respectable for a black tie event was a pair of dark trousers and a bowtie. So we rocked up, suitably attired for once. The event was in a giant ball room in one of the big international hotels on the bank of the great Nile river, and it oozed class. All of it high, at least until we arrived. We averaged it down somewhat.

We stood around awkwardly, amazed at the multiplicity of rowing blazers from our competitors, none more so than the subtle crimson of the huge Harvard Crew. Then there was the variety of local military uniforms bedecked with all manner of campaign insignia. Finally, sprinkled at random around this huge glittering room, the most sophisticated women any of us had ever seen, beautifully turned out in their long designer dresses. It was some show.

Looking at the ladies, even from a respectable distance, we began to understand why Richard Burton had married Cleopatra over and over again. We knew our literary stuff back then. Well, one of the crew was 'studying' English, and he briefed us. He told us 'married' was a euphemism. We didn't doubt it. They were all Cleopatras to us.

Feeling seriously uncomfortable amidst all these people, who were clearly far more in control of their life's direction than I was, I wandered across to an open window and gazed out at the famous busy river powering past the hotel. Even at that dark velvety evening time, the river was alive with traffic.

The big boats churned their way up and down seemingly without any lane protocols (it seemed to me thus perfectly emulating the rules of the local road system), and the smaller ones flitted around with sails or baby motors, darting to and fro across this historic waterway. It was impossible not to be struck by its majesty and intrigued by its action.

My marvelling and solo reverie were rudely inter-
rupted.

'I believe we have spoken on the telephone,' said the
Gruff Voice.

I turned around slowly, my brain getting into gear at
about the same speed as my entrails were turning to liquid. A well-built man in a most impressive uniform stood
looking sternly at me.

'My name is General Fayez Yakan,' he said loudly. 'I
have been a general for twenty years, and in that time, no
one has ever told me to eff off.'

He stopped and glared at me. The room was falling
silent. Clearly the night's entertainment was starting,
and I was cast as Clown Number One. I looked around
frantically. Where was Rory when I really needed him?
Not in sight.

'Oh mother,' I thought, 'here we go. Twenty years in
an Egyptian slammer.'

'Hello,' I squeaked and edgily backed away, desperately trying not to meet his eye.

When I did look up (it felt like a silent hour had
passed) Yakan was grinning from ear to ear.

'I must tell you,' he said, 'I get fed up with all the
fawning. It's a pleasure to meet someone who isn't impressed by my title.'

With that, he stuck out a large paw, crushed my damp
and shaking hand, and then steered me, weak kneed
with relief, across the room to what I discovered was the
remainder of the Rowing Federation. One by one they all
stepped up, grinning away, and clapped me on the back.

'Brave boy!' they said, followed by cackles of laughter. I think they really meant 'rude stupid child', but either way he had truly extracted his revenge.

I did meet him again two years later when I coached a later Trinity crew which also toured there. We very much enjoyed each other's company and I felt honoured when on leaving Egypt at the end of that second tour he presented me with a large blazer badge beautifully decorated with the insignia of the Suez Canal Authority, of which he was chairman at the time. I still wear it proudly on my rowing waistcoat.

But how did this all happen in the first place, I hear you ask? Well, it was all a series of dreadful accidents really.

But first, for anyone curious about some rowing terms, here is a short pictorial guide.

 CR   CR   CR

The Positions in a Rowing VIII

Traditionally, Bow (or 1) and 2 are regarded as technically the most proficient. Stroke (or 8) and 7 set the rate of strokes per minute and the resulting rhythm.

Those in the 3, 4, 5 and 6 seats comprise the 'engine room'. To be very rude, often 5 and 6 were deemed to be the engine room, and 3 and 4 regarded as merely sitting in for the ride ...

The reality with top crews, however, is that all eight crew members will be immensely fit and strong, will each have

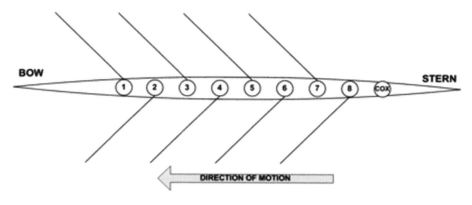

From the left, the Cox, Stroke with the fuzzy hair, 7, 6, 5, 4, 3, 2, and Bow with the white cap.

excellent rowing technique, and will also have an excellent feeling for a rhythm, alert to even minute variations in it.

On the following page is a modern eight racing shell, illustrating the shallow construction, and the fixed riggers on top into whose extremities the oars are locked when rowing.

Racing shells used for rowing are an extraordinary feat of engineering. They must be shallow to minimise water drag. In parallel, they need immense torsional strength to ensure that they don't twist longitudinally. They have to be light to maximise speed, and they have to be over 60 feet long to accommodate eight rowers and a steering coxswain.

Originally, they were constructed from cedar or other light-weight but strong wood. This however required additional load bearing struts, often kept in situ by brass screws. It wasn't long before the weight built up, such that all eight rowers would be required to carry the boat in and out of the water.

These days boats are constructed predominantly from fibre reinforced plastic, meaning they tend to be much lighter, stronger and hence faster. Typically, they can be carried easily by four rowers.

Given how shallow they have to be, and how long, not surprisingly they are fundamentally unstable. With an unskilled crew they will wobble atrociously from side to side with the poor rowers perched precariously on top. They rarely capsize, however, since the outstretched oars tend to prevent turtle impressions. Sinkings, however, where the boat is filled with water and forced below the surface by the resulting weight increase, are not uncommon. The boats have little protection even from small encroaching waves.

Falling out is rare, but it can happen if a severe 'crab' is caught by a rower. This occurs when the rower fails properly or 'cleanly' to extract the blade of the oar from the water at the end of the stroke. The oar blade can then slice downwards deep into the water. At the other end of the oar, the handle will lodge under the rower's arm.

Normally, this unfortunate event will cause a boat immediately to slew around to one side and end all forward motion. It is a catastrophic event during a race.

In extremis, a crab caught in a fast moving boat can lift the rower out of their seat, and deposit them in the water. And some would say, no more than they bloody well deserve, for losing concentration at a critical time...

As with the boats, the oars have changed over the years, not just in materials used, but also in shape. Originally they were long, slim and beautifully varnished wooden items. However they would bend under force when in use and were not that

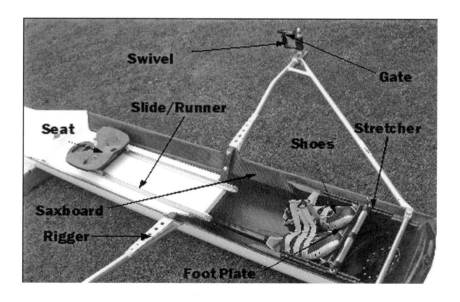

light. In common with the boats they serve, today oars are also made from artificial materials. They are immensely strong with larger 'spoons' at the water end and do not bend under pressure, despite what rowers will tell you.

Seat detailing. Each of the seats in a racing shell is as depicted in the photograph. Each rower's seat will move forward and back on the slide/runner during each stroke. The shoes are screwed into the boat but must have quick release straps in case of a sinking.

Finally, there are two types of rowing. What one normally associates with rowing is known as 'sweep' rowing, namely each rower has one oar. Sweep rowing can be done in pairs, fours (IVs) or eights (VIIIs).

'Sculling' is where each rower has two (smaller) oars. There are octuple sculls around, which have eight rowers with two sculling blades each and which resemble giant egg beaters, but the most common sculling boats are the single, double and quad.

Doubles and quads can have reasonable human beings forming the crews, but single scullers are usually complete nutters. They resemble goalkeepers in football. A law onto themselves. This comes from the fact that single sculling boats can capsize readily, and hence over the years single scullers ingest so much water that their brains go soggy. This is my scientific analysis after years of careful observation.

CR   CR   CR

Cast of Characters

(Being the 1977 Trinity Crew)

Cox – Jarlath McGee

Never the slimmest of gents to fulfil that role (I always thought he put the 'w' into an eight), he had a natural authority, a strong voice, he could read a race, and with eight obvious exceptions, he didn't otherwise suffer fools. Actually, there were days when he didn't suffer anyone.

His way with the ladies was legendary (there was a clue in his title), but it never interfered with his boat driving. Boy, could he steer a straight line. River courses can disguise the steering inability of a cox, but straight rowing courses leave no hiding room for boat drivers who fail to spot that there are no bends. Jarlath's command of a boat left nothing to be desired.

Stroke – John Macken

The Boss. John had rowed at school, and had been around the Club for a couple of years before most of the rest of us showed up. We never really saw him much in the first term of each year. He claimed his engineering studies were so onerous that he had to cover all three terms in the first semester so he could row during the remaining two. We didn't believe a word of it.

Problem was, we couldn't do without the bugger. Every time he sat into the stroke seat (usually displacing the author) there was unanimity that the boat just went much faster. And you should have seen him in a single sculling boat. Actually, you would never have seen him had you been in the same race. He was just gone.

Best known phrase? 'Slow fuckin' down', which was all too regularly growled at the engine room behind him every time we crashed up the slide for the next stroke, utterly destroying his carefully wrought rhythm.

7 – Rory Reilly

At 25, Rory was one of the more mature members of the senior rowing squad, if that's not an oxymoron. Actually it is. In addition to being incredibly old, however, at 6 feet 4 inches and lean with it, he was the perfect rowing shape. What was worse, despite not having rowed before coming to university, he turned out to be a natural.

By Year Final the author knew him well. Too well. As things turned out, this would be a third year in a row in which he would again sit behind him in a boat, becoming far too familiar with every wrinkle and hair on the back of his neck. Ugh. He was supposed to be 'studying' Advanced Colouring In, otherwise known as Geology. Or maybe it was Geography. Either way, it involved lots of drawings and little else.

Favourite phrase? 'Talk to me cox,' when dying in a race.

6 – The Author

Possibly one of the finest oarsmen ever to join the Boat Club, his rowing ability was exceeded only by his self-delusion. The latter is world class. Otherwise, nothing to see here. Next please.

5 – Dave Weale

Dave had been to a minor English public school, although he usually forgot to mention the minor bit. This was to distinguish himself from those of us who, he informed us, had merely been told stories in the local hedge schools by way of an education. At 6 feet, 5 inches, lean and blond, he thought he might be every girl's dream. We disagreed but couldn't risk him being right, so we concluded that he had to be chopped down at every opportunity. This book is no different.

Most of his time in Trinity was spent scanning the daily visitors coming round the tourist track ('say, do you know where Kelly's book is') in a desperate attempt to spot the Hollywood producer who would give him his big break. ('I could be the new Redford, man.') Yeah, right Dave. Meantime, just pull harder on the damn oar.

In fairness, he could row. He was probably the best in the crew at it, so much so that one of the coaches christened him our 'Baby East German', after the Blond Beasts from the East who seemed to be winning everything in those 'amateur' days.

Favourite phrase? 'It's cool, man.' And sometimes it was, but we were never going to tell him.

4 – James Murnane

James was a phenomenon. He appeared in the novice squad towards the end of Year One and was co-opted straight into the top senior boat. Immensely strong and seemingly quite unable to row at anything other than full pressure at all times, he parked himself in the 4 seat and owned it for two straight years.

His one failing was his appetite. If it stopped moving, he ate it. Sometimes it didn't even get to stop moving. You could see the nervousness on the face of the ducks as they swam past the Boat House. One pause for breath and the orange sauce would have been out. Favourite phrase? 'Oh yes please, I will have just one more.' No wonder his nickname was 'Munch'.

3 – Dave Sanfey

The second survivor of rowing for several years before the author and his fellow novices arrived. The pedigree showed in the smoothness and consistency of his rowing. He took over the captaincy of the Club for Year Two and his professionalism and determination set the example for anyone tempted to underestimate the commitment needed for rowing.

But what really set him apart was that you knew he would never, ever, give up. A man with whom to share a trench when the war started. Mind you, the trench would have needed a TV so that he could watch the BBC test card to which he seemed at times addicted. No, I don't know either.

2 – Ted O'Morchoe

Arriving to slot into the crew in Year Final, he constituted the only change from Year Two. A cultured oar, having rowed successfully at schoolboy level, he slipped smoothly into the 2 seat and stayed well away from any trouble. In fact, there were days when he seemed to be utterly invisible until, that is, you noticed the puddle coming past you at the end of the stroke. As neat, powerful and tidy as you could wish for.

Sadly, though, he was another engineer and so lived in a theoretical world few of us could comprehend. Well born and well brought up, though he only let it show occasionally, such as in his favourite phrase, 'Baxter's Royal Game Soup would go down very well.'

Bow – Kieran Mulcahy

By far the strongest man in the club, and another natural rower, he was the one man with whom the author ended up rowing (as in flowing), and occasionally rowing (as in thumping), every year for five years.

Of course, the author didn't know that when he first laid eyes on him. Which was one day when Kieran arrived for weight training. Within a couple of minutes it became obvious that he could lift anything in the weights room. Actually, he could lift everything in the weights room, and usually did.

He could have lifted the back of a bus. He could have lifted the front of the bus. Come to think of it, if only they had built them a little shorter, he could have lifted the entire damn bus. Nonetheless, for a big man, he proved adept at providing the balance and subtlety required in the bow seat of every boat he sat in.

Favourite phrase? 'The fuckin' East Germans.'

What a crew. Enough material there for decade's worth of psychiatric analysis.

Year Zero

Why on Earth Go to University?

How random is your life? The school Prior came into the classroom unannounced one morning in my final year of secondary school. It was a private religious school in Dublin and not cheap for my parents, Dad being on the salary of a middle ranking bank official. In Ireland in those days banks pretty much guaranteed a job for life, they were prestigious employers, and they provided a decent pension. So plenty of attractions in a time of economic impoverishment.

However the salary levels were very modest and bonuses hadn't yet crossed the Atlantic. Rising through the ranks of the bank every few years was good for Dad's career, but not good for his children's education, as promotion invariably involved a move to yet another town, which in turn meant my siblings and I were yanked out of the place where we were just settling in. Ultimately, we were mostly all packed off to boarding school from our early teen years to try to get some continuity and possibly even academic success before finishing our education.

At least that's what we were told. Alternatively, five children heading into teen times might have been a bit too boisterous for our Mother but, either way, off we were sent. I was despatched to Terenure College, which was usually regarded as one of Dublin's two rugby academies. That was quite unfortunate as I didn't play rugby. Actually, I didn't play any sport and since there was bugger all else to do, I studied. Hence I finished up in the A class or 'swot stream'.

The Prior distributed a form to each of us that morning. He didn't bother distributing them to the other three 'non swot' streams. He probably reckoned that as they all played rugby they wouldn't do any studying. Staggering how the whims of one man can form Normal People, as you might say.

As I looked at it, it seemed to be an application form to go and study at Trinity College, then the major unit within Dublin University. I had no intention of going to university, but the Prior was not a man to cross, and so I dutifully filled in the blanks, signed the form, and passed it back.

Unbeknownst to me, he reappeared the following day with forms for the other local option, University College Dublin (UCD). As I was in the infirmary that morning with boy flu, I didn't see or get that form, and no one thought to mention it.

Unbeknownst to the Prior, he had changed my life.

Later in August that year I was in London working a summer job as a barman in a giant pub, which still revels in the utterly misleading name of The Crown Hotel, Cricklewood. It was indeed in Cricklewood but it was less of a 'Crown Hotel' and more of a convenient location for heavy weekend drinking and fighting. I wouldn't necessarily call it unduly rough. 'War zone' would be a better description. Some nights it made the parallel uncivil antics in Beirut seem positively genteel. Everyone knew when trouble started that there was no sense in calling the police. They had more sense than to get within range even sitting within their brightly coloured panda cars. And as for getting out of the cars? No chance.

Quite often on Saturday nights we didn't bother locking the doors since anyone who wanted to enter after closing time could simply climb through the smashed windows. I suspected the local glaziers had some of the regular drinkers on retainers. And I will not describe what entertainment the manager laid on to avoid the otherwise quiet Sunday afternoons, save to say that Monday's *Sun* newspaper was always scoured to see whether the same ladies had made a second appearance in the lives of the attendees. What a place to land in, straight out of a straight school.

Meantime, back in 'normality', a letter had arrived for me at our then home in the middle of Ireland. Dad wrote and told me I had been offered a place at Trinity and would I like to go? I hadn't given it any thought. Frankly, I had little idea what university life would mean. If it resembled school, I would be bored rigid. He said that if I worked in the Easter and summer breaks to make enough money to live on, he would pay the fees. I got the feeling he thought I should go, and having little idea what else I might do other than escape the life of a barman in a human zoo, I agreed.

Why on Earth Sit in a Rowing Boat?

So, in late September 1973, I walked slowly for the first time through the gates of Trinity College, passing the front building housing the Porters' Lodge, and out on to the wide central cobbled path leading into the Front Square quadrangle. With the Chapel on one side, and the similarly sized Exam Hall on the other, it was a perfect balance of classic architecture exuding taste without being overly dominant. I felt immediately uncomfortable. How on earth could I ever fit into a place like this?

It was Freshers' Week, resulting in Front Square being festooned with all manner of clubs and societies seeking to attract new members. I managed to avoid them all as I sidled past, too shy and scared to speak to the confident and clearly very mature students pressing the merits of their particular fetishes on the fresh student meat.

It was then I saw it. A beautifully varnished wooden boat sitting upright on a pair of supporting trestle slings, with equally well presented wooden oars set balanced on either side. Over the years in the bank, my father built much of the family furniture – there being little money for such frivolities – and one winter, with me getting in his way, he built a two-man canoe from plywood and canvas. I remembered his advice about spotting good cabinet making, which was to check that all the screws faced precisely the same direction along the major spine of the finished item.

Intrigued by the boat, I went over to look more closely, and sure enough, each of the hundred or more brass screws all faced the same line. It seemed beautifully built.

Freshers' Week at Trinity College

I had turned away when a voice said, 'You could sit in it at the weekend if you like.'

The voice came from a tall Smiling Man. Another man who was to change my life.

'Why would I want to do that?' I replied a little too aggressively.

'Because I think you might be good at it, and I think you might enjoy it,' came the smiling reply.

I dropped the aggression and responded weakly, 'I've never done it before,' I pleaded, and, 'I'm not really very fit nor very strong,' I continued to protest.

At the time I was just about 6 feet tall and weighed almost 11 stone.

'Doesn't matter,' he said, 'we'll get you fit and strong. Nine o'clock at Islandbridge on Saturday, see you there.'

He moved across to another victim, and I slipped out of his sight. Waking early on the Saturday I thought a bit about the Smiling Man and, recognising that I had nothing else to do that weekend, decided that I might as well go and look at Islandbridge rowing so that I could rule it out on the basis of fact. So I got on my bike and pedalled off to the Boat House.

He was there.

'My name is Tom Noble,' said the Smiling Man, 'and here are your boats.'

If ever a man were blessed with an appropriate surname, it was Tom. After Trinity he devoted his life to creating nondenominational schools in Northern Ireland against a background where this was very unusual, and often strenuously resisted, by less so-called Christian folk, unable or unwilling to dig themselves out of their hundred-year-old redoubts.

Meantime, Tom was Admiral in the Boat Club, meaning he had been Captain the previous year. He oversaw the novices, or 'maidens' as we were properly, and accurately, known, and promptly turned us over to the two coaches.

A Most Personable Coach

Brian Persson had been brought up in southern Africa, his Swedish forbears having moved there generations back, presumably to get warm. Tall, well-built and strong, he had this wonderful languid African style about him. Nothing seemed to faze him, and he had a fine rowing pedigree, as evidenced by his picture on the wall of the Long Room.

The Boat House at Islandbridge

This glorious room is positioned right across the entire length of the first floor of the Trinity Boat House. From two sides, which are virtually fully glazed, it looks up and down the Liffey at one of its loveliest points. The walls were, and remain, bedecked with photos of past crews, together with beautifully varnished oars, some dating back over a century. It is a fascinating store of rowing memories. Brian was up there with the best of them.

Stories circulated that he had also rowed successfully in South Africa until a frightful car crash rearranged most of his limbs and organs. He had obviously mostly recovered, and to me he seemed a relaxed, comfortably mature figure who treated us arriving maidens with a tolerant and benevolent manner.

Critically, for the first time in my short life, I felt I wasn't being patronised. Coming from a school where I was used to being addressed as 'what is it now wretch?' it was refreshing. So I tried early to ingratiate myself with him.

'I have a great aunt in Nyasaland,' I said, suddenly remembering the brightly coloured stamps on letters to my Mother sent regularly by her overseas relative. Not that I had the slightest clue as to where in that vast Continent the little country actually sat.

'Small world,' said Brian with a grin. 'I live in Dublin.' Well that worked well.

Islandbridge

Dublin University Boat Club is located alone on the south bank of the Liffey, opposite the first weir some two miles upriver from the city centre. It sits adjacent to the Irish National War Memorial Gardens, a surprisingly serene Lutyens design commemorating the near 50,000 Irish men and women killed in the First World War.

The Gardens took a time to be set up after the war to end all wars (it can only have been a politician who provided that label), considering the mixed nationalist feelings around in those days. Then a certain Major General Bernard Hickie got involved. He finished the project and the Gardens were unofficially and quietly opened in 1938. He couldn't spell his surname properly, but he built a fine memorial.

Overlooking it high up on the other side of the river stands the Wellington Monument, situated on the southern side of the Phoenix Park. Although not so proud of it in later years, the man on the column had been born in Dublin. He married a member of the Longford family which was amusing as that was the town in the Midlands where my parents were then living. Not sure we knew her though. But it did set me thinking that perhaps these two proximities might together constitute enough remote connections for me not to be too quick to dismiss this rowing stuff.

Months later, when rowing below and between these great reminders of serious history, complaining to Brian that I was 'dying in the boat' never did seem to carry much weight with him. Plainly he was well aware of the Iron Duke glowering down from one side of the river, and Rupert Brooke's war verses susurrating across from the other. Obviously there is 'dying', and then there is dying.

(Rowing the Dublin Head of the River race each year, down below the first weir and under the various bridges straddling the lower Liffey, the joke always was that passing under the first bridge you felt that you were going to die, and as you shot out the other side your realised to your absolute horror you were *not* going to die, but instead you were going to have to finish the race...).

An Lar

The buses out that way mostly all head into, and sometimes out the other side of, Dublin city centre. You can tell that from the helpful rotating destination sign on the front of the vehicle which says 'An Lar', being

Irish for 'centre'. The bus signage was designed by a real comedian. When the route actually terminates in the centre, the signage says, 'An Lar, via An Lar'. It is a helpful reminder to tourists that they should seek to learn the local language at the earliest opportunity, after they have worked out where the hell Dublin has got to.

The other local rowing clubs are located on the north bank, but all share the narrow twisting one mile rowing stretch of Dublin's bisecting water. It is a pleasant reach with no non-rowing buildings visible throughout virtually all of it. It is usually quite calm, being protected by overhanging trees and vegetation, and the higher surrounding ground. It is not manicured; there is a rough winding and sometimes very narrow towpath on one side which rises and falls with the contours of the adjacent bank. In places it has been carefully crafted to deposit inattentive rowing coaches, and their accompanying bicycles, directly into the water.

The river itself widens and narrows but always with plenty of warning. Its course has remained unchanged for decades of oarsmen and women and it is probably that familiarity which continues to draw its rowing graduates back year after year to reminisce about their happy young days.

The First Noel

Arriving there on the first morning it seemed I was deep in the Irish countryside and not at all in the 'burbs of An Lar. Despite all that, had that first day been windy, wet or cold I doubt whether I would have returned. A bleak mid-autumn drenching would have done nothing for me. I had had enough of those at various homes in the West and the Midlands of the country, where often it seemed as if there was nothing out there other than fog and water, boredom and bog.

As it happened, that day was the reverse. The autumn morning air was warm and sunny. The leaves on the surrounding trees were just starting to turn. The river was flowing gently past the landing slip without ripple or fuss. There was a nervous and excitable chatter from the group of new recruits clustered around the boats resting on their slings, waiting to be allocated a seat. It was truly a beautiful day in a beautiful location. It struck me that maybe a page was being turned in my life.

Such a shame then to have it spoiled by having to clamber into a boat feeling half terrified about the likelihood of an early swim. Racing shells are not wide and require a set of balanced oars to avoid an immediate flip. Looking at the first maiden boat edging away from the slip, it seemed to me that the eight souls perched in it were sitting very high off the water, in a naturally unbalanced state, and would doubtless get a ducking.

My turn came, and the other maiden coach, Noel Graham, took control. We were allocated a boat known as *Hazel*. Given its undoubted age, vast weight and 'collectors' condition, it was obvious to me that this was a most historic artefact. Clearly it had served previously as a tender to Noah's Ark. Noel, by contrast, was somewhat younger, though still a very experienced cox, who would go on in that role to represent Ireland in the 1976 Montreal Olympics.

He despatched me to a seat in the middle of the second boat and, with seven others like me struggling to settle in, he hopped into the cox's seat. Such bravery. Once we figured out which way to face, which not everyone got right first time, the boat was pushed out from the landing slip and into the river, and we tried to set off upstream.

I'm not sure how far we travelled. Brian told us afterwards that we seemed to resemble nothing more than eight pale maidens battering the surrounding water into submission, occasionally causing the poor suffering conveyance to move vaguely upriver.

There being no electronic speaker systems for the cox to communicate with the crew in those days (well, at least not in our boats), he or she simply bellowed out the instructions. I wasn't conscious of Noel saying anything on the upriver stretch of that first outing. Frankly, I wasn't conscious of anything at all except the sudden appearance of monster blisters on my hands and red marks on my bare knees as I continually whacked the oar against them in a futile attempt to race the oar handle up the slide in time to take the next stroke.

(Time on the slide is time wasted someone said, before we went out on the water – he was truly evil, whoever he was.) Either way, I kept losing that battle (some would say it's a war I never won) and my knees got more and more battered. Later, as we all eventually tired and lost our initial fright, things calmed down a little and the boat seemed to move a little more smoothly.

It was then I heard Noel wail out, 'Lucy, Lucy,' a cry he returned to several times on that first return trip back down river to the slip where we alighted. I felt for the fellow, clearly missing a fine lady, but apart from that oddity, he too seemed very friendly and decent.

The blisters. Oh the blisters. Enough material for a full term of undergraduate medical analysis. Red and white ones filled with water. Black and blue ones filled with blood. Yellow ones, the really bad bastards, filled with pus having gone septic. Burst ones. Half burst ones. On both palms. On every finger. I had no idea that my hands could be so soft. Had Pol Pot been the coach, he would have murdered the lot of us for being idle intelligentsia.

Somebody advised toughening them up with methylated spirits (the hands, that is, not the intelligentsia). I'm still looking for him. Dear God did that ridiculous 'remedy' sting. And just as the blisters were starting to heal by the Friday after the preceding weekend, the following day we started all over again. I got blisters on blisters. It took maybe a decade after I last held an oar before the physical scars faded away. I can still remember the pain of the first few strokes each Saturday morning. And I was doing this for fun?

Early Capture

Reality about the real brutality of rowing dawned early on when, after a few weeks, the thirty or so of us maidens were called into the Long Room and the names of those forming the first crew were called out. Mine was not amongst them.

'I guess that means the rest of us are just the dregs,' came O'Neill's cynical voice from the rear of the bunch, also omitted from first choice. Funny how he became known as Dregs O'Neill thereafter.

Dregs or not, rowing in the oldest, most decrepit wooden clinker lump of a boat or not, with no proper kit, with stinging hands and sore knees, it mattered not. Something clicked, in addition to my aching back.

Maybe it was the people. Maybe it was the structured life around the training regime. Perhaps it was the drawing out of an innate competitive spirit dormant until then. Maybe all of these in part. It doesn't really matter, and I don't really know. Actually, I don't really care what the psychological answer might be. I loved it. That was enough.

I had a focus, an extraordinary mix of fellow oarsmen to get to know, an excuse to get fit, plus the river was something special. Always different, always moving, sometimes challenging, mostly calming, it became our mistress, master, slave and lover, all rolled into one. I was wedded to it after a month.

I never did make that first maiden crew. Some kindly say it was because I had mentioned early on that I would not be available for the Maiden Championships in July, as I was going to New York to work for money to live the following year. I had a suspicion however that it was really because I was too unfit, and too skinny. Chicken legs don't do it in rowing.

Lycra-Free Life

We had no proper kit in those days. Some of us didn't even have improper kit. Most of us wore tired old dogs of once white Dunlop Green Flash gym shoes which slotted into leather straps fixed (supposedly) into the boats. These days the shoes are built into the boat. In those days you brought your own, rather like cheap wine to a stranger's party.

The Green descriptor was pretty accurate given the usual age of the old dogs, but the Flash bit always perplexed me. Heading further up the body, woolly, grey and baggy old gym shorts, topped off with cotton t-shirts and an old family heirloom sweater or sweatshirt on top, completed the look. All in all, it was the sort of stuff that you'd be too embarrassed to leave at a charity shop these days.

In wintertime, this sartorial get-up meant that if you weren't having your nuts frozen off, and often even if you were, you were spending most of your time in the chemist shop hunting out Vaseline to rub into the red train tracks gouged in your soft white flesh by the inch thick, half-finished rough seams in the utterly inappropriate shorts. And the clothes themselves were worse than useless for keeping out the cold and damp. We would all have contracted hypothermia, had it been invented back then.

Each year the new arrivals into the club included a few escaping rugby buggers. You could pick them out instantly. They had their old school rugby shirts, tough old rugby shorts and thick long socks which prevented their calves from being sliced open each rowing outing by the naked metal edges of the slide channels positioned under the moving seats. Softies.

Lycra hadn't yet appeared, thank goodness, but in any event in those days it would have been confused with those black outfits reputedly available for hard cash down Soho way of a Friday evening. And now everyone wears the stuff, bursting out all over, just like Rogers and Hammerstein's 'June'. Yeuch.

Why on Earth Start Training?

We got introduced into fitness training. For some, like me, this was a first. We were supposed to run around the Trinity campus during the dark autumn and winter each Monday and Wednesday evening. In addition, we were supposed to do 'heavy' weights on a Tuesday and 'speed' weights on a Thursday. In my case there wasn't much difference between the two. When I started I couldn't do a push up of my own weight, never mind anything more.

Running training was also troublesome for me. I could sprint for a bus, but I could never run properly, so having to run in darkness was a blessing. No one could see. I plodded around desperately trying not to come last. The main thing was never to stop, no matter how hard it seemed. Even then it was dawning on us that in rowing you just had to keep going. There was, and is, no alternative once you set off.

The heavy weights session involved going into the college boiler room and competing for space with the main boiler (which had clearly been liberated from Stephenson's Rocket a century previously). It was dirty, dusty and cold. Trinity students obviously required no heating during the daytime. There were some rusty barbells lying around on the rough concrete floor, and an old wooden bench for sleeping on overnight if you lost your keys to your college rooms. That was it. All in all, today's 'Elf and Safey' would have condemned it quicker than a teenager moving a thumb on a Gameboy consol.

As for the actual weight training itself, we had no idea, and so initially we tended to stand around and occasionally move a barbell from one location to another while providing everyone present with valuable views on the world's events of the day.

As we continued to train, however, these sessions started to become competitive and so the talking got replaced by grunting and crashing as we hoiked up the bars and let them fall suddenly, hoping the noise would suggest we were trying hard and matching each other.

I found it really hard. In those early days, there were a few shorter fellows around. They could really shift the metal. It eventually dawned on the remainder of us long(ish) weaklings that they were always going to be able to lift more than us because they had less distance to travel when doing squats or bench presses. So there was no point in competing between people.

And so we started tracking our own progress and thus blundered into the only way to do weight training properly, which is to measure your own progress and ignore the puffers and grunters elsewhere. Once we had figured that out, and as the years went on, it was no surprise that we all got a lot stronger. Weight, or resistance, training really does work, and actually should continue forever, even when not rowing.

As for the actual rowing, that was what Saturday mornings were for. When I say 'rowing' it really meant that, early in the season, random VIIIs would be selected from whoever happened to turn up. The resulting crews were rough, having an extraordinary mix of cultured former school rowers, semi-fit refugees from rugby or other sports, and some rank beginners. And some were very rank.

Given that it was the first year of rowing for most of us, there was of course a total dearth of power and co-ordination as we tried to pull the oars through the water. Brian used to say we were so weak that we weren't capable of pulling a soldier off our sister, or the skin off a rice pudding. I didn't understand either comment. I was sure my sisters didn't know any soldiers and I was always so hungry my tins of Ambrosia Creamed Rice never got the chance to develop a skin.

As the year progressed, however, the numbers attending the mid-week training sessions dropped off steadily, and so it was with the rowing attendees. By Christmas we were down to two crews of eight each. Many of the lads were never going to make it as serious oarsmen. Some would fail as they could simply not grasp how to move a boat in unison with others. Some were simply not built for it physically. Some thought it too boring. Some thought it too hard. Some refused to prioritise training over study obligations, beer, girls or all of the above.

But as the year went on, and as it became obvious to all who would make the first novice boat and who would not, I began to admire those (like me of course) who stuck at it despite knowing full well they would be in the second boat at best.

Some really liked the time discipline imposed by the training regime. Some liked the fitness buzz. Some just liked the water. Some liked the regular verbal abuse, euphemistically called 'camaraderie'. In truth, however, once the outliers fell away, many of those remaining formed lifelong friendships regardless of their rowing prowess. There was indeed some true camaraderie.

I was always grateful to them, though, since otherwise I might not have been able to row at all.

In parallel I was discovering a few things about rowing. It imposes structure, even on non-Olympic amateurs looking to compete. Getting to training, completing the session, getting changed and showered afterwards, and then refuelling altogether takes anything from three to four hours daily. Structuring this around university lectures and related studies and sleeping and eating altogether leaves little room for much else. Tough for many. Ideal for me as it was keeping my dreaded boredom away.

Trial VIIIs

This annual event, at which the Trinity crews for the forthcoming racing season would be announced, constituted the first training break of the new calendar year. It was, and is still to this day, held in the Boat House Long Room at Islandbridge, and comprises drinks followed by a dinner after which new selected crew members or 'colours' are obliged to stand up and recite or sing a party piece. It tends to get a bit raucous. Volunteers were called for in my first year to assist in serving pints from the bar.

Not being an alcohol man until I started down that wondrous path the following year, and having worked in pubs, I said I would help out. I didn't drink due, I guess, to having 'enjoyed' something of a strict upbringing, between hardworking and very strict (though loving) parents, and an academic education via the hard and sometimes brutal Christian Brothers, followed by the Carmelite order. The latter were much less severe, but no less narrowly focussed. There hadn't been much by way of disrespect, unruliness and certainly no anarchy in my life. Besides beer was expensive, and so I left it alone.

In Year Zero, my first Trial VIIIs, virtually everyone was drinking Guinness before dinner, which meant keeping pints poured and 'topped up' as orders were placed. That year I turned out to be the only volunteer serving some fifty thirsty souls and so I was moving frantically to keep up.

At one stage, Tom Noble wandered up with a glazed look and, as I was pouring yet more pints, he politely asked me how my rowing was coming along. We chatted while I worked but plainly my concentration wandered. When I passed his ordered pint to him, he looked at me quizzically and asked whether my father had been a bishop. I looked at him completely blankly. Mind you, after a few pints on an empty stomach, he was looking a bit blank himself.

Inclining his head toward the fresh pint, I saw what he meant. The creamy head was twice the proper depth. Apologising, I took it back and topped it up properly with the black stuff. Smiling again, he thanked me profusely, turned, walked across and behind Roger White, a fellow new recruit. He pulled Roger's shirt away from his neck, and attempted to empty the pint into the gap. Roger quickly twisted away and responded with a shriek and a laugh. It seemed perfectly normal behaviour to both of them. No wonder the girls thought we were freaks. We were.

Meantime, I spied Noel heading towards me, obviously needing a drink.

'Two pints please Dave,' and I duly (and carefully this time) topped off two pints of Guinness and passed them to him.

At the same time I said, 'I'm sorry about Lucy,' and looked sympathetically at him.

He looked back at me through a Guinness haze. 'Wha? Who?'

I said 'Lucy, Lucy' a little more loudly.

He shook his head in confusion, said 'Thanks Dave,' and walked away.

Rory was within hearing distance.

'What's with this Lucy stuff, Dave?'

I said, 'poor old Noel calls out for this girl every so often during the outings, obviously something dreadful has happened.'

'Dave, Dave,' said Rory shaking his head sorrowfully, 'how the fuck did you ever get into university?'

'What are you talking about.'

'He's not saying Lucy, you moron, he's saying "loosely". It means would you fucking relax in the boat.'

I really did need to start drinking. Let's face it, I had to do something by way of an education.

Training Break

I got home for the Christmas fortnight, which was to the aforementioned Longford, situated in the middle of the country. Being the local bank manager, Dad was very popular with the farmers and small industry operators, provided that he had approved their loan applications. This gratitude was always on display at Christmas time.

That year he decided to accept an invitation to drinks out at a big local farmer's house well out in the countryside. He suggested that I join him. Actually, I suspect it was really Mother deciding that he would need a chaperone, and she was hardly going to go out to some farmer's house to be offered a glass of milk while she listened to the men tell farming war stories over a decent bottle of whiskey. So I was despatched.

It didn't start or finish well. The bank house was on the main street and Dad's car was always parked inside the gates below the house and facing out at street level. This being Christmas Eve, there was the ubiquitous white van parked fully across the gates.

'I've got this,' said Dad. 'Watch, listen and learn.'

We went into the adjacent building, which was a very dark and very long bar, with a full line of fellows drinking bottles of Guinness Stout. The air was thick with cigarette smoke and growling conversation.

'Who owns that nice white van parked outside my gates?' asked Dad in a loud voice and with a big smile.

There was an uncomfortably long silence before a voice at the end of the bar answered.

'Allied Oirish Fukin' Finance owns it,' said the voice, 'an Oi'm too fukin' pissed to move it.' End of.

Exit two stout-free parties back on to the street.

The rain had started for the second time that week. The first time it had lasted three days and so I figured this time it would be down for four days. Now however it was coming down in stair rods. It was so hard it almost hurt to stand out in it.

'Never mind,' said Dad, 'we'll take a taxi.'

And so I spent the most boring two hours of my life drinking the milk Mother would have been given while listening to two men happily discussing interest rates for agricultural loans.

At length, Dad rose, and rather less steadily his host also made his way towards the vertical.

'Oi'll drive yez home,' he said.

Dad said politely that he was most grateful, while simultaneously pleading desperately for a taxi only to be told there was no phone in the house.

'Leasht I can do,' said the farmer, 'after all dem loans you went an' gave me.'

The Volks Meets the Ditch

And so the three of us piled into a Volkswagen Beetle that looked for all the world as if it had been Ferry Porsche's first wheelie child. Dad was told to get into the back seat. Clearly the farmer regarded him as a rather more valuable commodity than the silent lump of a milk-sucking son he had brought with him.

I wasn't unduly bothered at this allocation. The rear seat smelt like the family pig had found a drier alternative to his usual preferred external lavatory spot. As for me, since I was clearly expendable I got the death seat. At least it had a roof, I thought, as the rain pounded down. Much more of it and Noah's old tender *Hazel* would be called into a different form of action.

Peering forward through the windscreen wondering how on earth anyone could see anything, I got a bang on the arm and looked across to see the farmer passing me both ends of a piece of string.

'Hol' dat,' he said.

Reaching across me, he opened the front quarter glass on the door of the car. The rain now came in at my side and blew across the windscreen from the inside. At least now it was being washed evenly from both sides.

'Roight,' he said, 'now pull dem lads.'

Looking at him in complete confusion, he motioned his hands in parallel one way and then the other. I got it, and dutifully pulled the string ends, first to one side and then to the other. Detecting some faint external movement out of the corner of my eye, I looked up at the windscreen and saw what appeared to be some manner of single wiping mechanism moving a few inches either side of the vertical, directly in front of the farmer.

This item seemed to me to be doing an excellent job of smearing the windscreen and clearing the rain for all of a millisecond before it filled again. The string went out both quarter glasses, looped around the wiper, and was motorised by the milk sucker. At least that's what I think the farmer called me but he might have got his consonants mixed up.

'Grand job,' I was told, 'there's hope for ya yet,' as the unbelievable clatter of the vintage air-cooled engine started up and we set off out into the black night.

'If it wasn't for ya, I'd have ta do dat meself,' the farmer yelled happily at me, 'an dat might be a bit dodgy while drivin'.'

I tended to agree until I noticed that he was concentrating furiously on getting both hands free of the steering wheel to extract tobacco from a tightly closed tin of the finest Balkan Sobranje, and then trying to fill a pipe with it. I could tell he was concentrating furiously since his tongue was halfway out of his mouth. Meanwhile, the steering wheel was being more or less manoeuvred by his thighs. Mostly less.

There were no streetlights on the lane out from the farm. There were no streetlights on the tar road which meandered gradually from the lane towards the main Mullingar/Longford road, and there were no streetlights on that thoroughfare either.

Worse, it became obvious quite quickly that there were no lights on the car, if you excluded the two candles well hidden behind the glass on the pair of 'headlamps'. Mind you, the rain was lashing the windscreen to such an extent I'm not sure lights would have made any difference.

There was a deep ditch either side of us. I decided my death would be easier if I didn't see the chosen ditch coming my way so I closed my eyes. I kept on pulling the string this way and that. I wasn't sure why I was bothering. I felt a little like famous Lady Astor asking for ice in her cocktail as the berg ripped through the *Titanic*. A little pointless you might say.

I've no idea how we got down the track to the tar road. I guess the car knew the way. I have even less idea how we managed to stay on the tar road heading towards the main road without being welcomed by any of the deep ditches on either side. We seemed to be surviving somehow. Time dragged. I kept pulling the string. It was comforting, if pointless.

We had got most of the way towards the main road before there was a large bang and the car suddenly stopped. I thought we had hit a cow but Dad, who to my surprise was wide awake in the rear, said, 'that might have been someone.' Dad was very subtle when he needed to be, and I knew immediately that 'might' meant 'definitely was'.

The awful clattering ceased as the engine died. Warily, we all got out, being careful to avoid sliding into the surrounding ditches. I didn't actually need to be that careful as the ditch on my side was already filled. It started swearing and gradually it revealed a sodden chappie clawing his way out of it.

'Lookat what yave done ya dangerous Cee U Next Tuesday,' said the sodden chappie (except he shortened it to the capital letters).

He stood, after a fashion, forlorn and swaying under his tweed cap, and pulled up the collar of a long coat tied around the waist with thick twine. Whoever held the Irish rights to rope products in those days would have lived well, what with all the engineering and fashion applications available.

We all apologised and the farmer asked him whether he was all right.

'Only Oi've no tax or insurance, I'd sue ya, ya bollix.'

'Tanx be to Jaysus for dat,' came the farmer's response, 'shore I've none eider.'

The sodden chappie was working himself up somewhat.

'Look at me bike, its feckin' ruined', and sure enough there seemed to be the mortal remains of a once Nifty Honda Fifty poking out from the large brackish puddle at the bottom of said ditch.

'Get in the car and Oi'll get ya home if there's no more complainin'.'

And so Dad found himself sharing the lavatorial back seat as the awful air-cooled cacophony started up, and again the two ends of the piece of string were passed to me. Surely, I thought to myself, it had clearly just been clinically proven that the mechanism was about as useful as smoke signals in a hurricane. But no.

'Pull away there,' came the instruction and we trundled off towards what passed for civilisation in those parts, in those days.

'How was it?' Mother asked when we finally got in and Dad had retired for the night.

'You wouldn't believe what happened,' I replied.

'Really?' she said with a grin, and I suddenly realised how far ahead of the game she really was.

Mind you, she had form with driving, that Mother of ours. Dad drove Alfa Romeos, but badly. He always seemed to want to get into the top gear at the slowest speed, and the poor old Italian thoroughbreds never got to fill their lungs. Until, that was, Mother drove them. She took every gear to the red line on the rev counter before she would change up. You could almost hear the excitement in the car's engine as she climbed into the driver's seat to take control.

She commanded those cars in other ways as well. One year, driving a happy bunch of revellers home after a New Years' party, Mother in the hard charging Alfa was flagged down by the gardaí. Advancing suspiciously, the Sergeant (she always promoted the policemen she met) invited her to lower the window and there was a conversation designed to test her sobriety. The final question put to her was, 'and what is the registration of the car Madam?'

Addressing him as one would a small but slow learning child, she replied that if he took himself around to the front of the car he could answer his own question. After a long, thoughtful stare at her, she was waved on.

Race Time

I escaped back to the relative normality of university. I was starting to settle in and I could see that without too much effort I might be able to slide through the end of year exams. So I could keep on rowing.

After that Christmas, Brian and Noel stuck me in the stroke seat of the Maiden B crew. At first I wasn't really bothered. I was just rowing along minding my own business and I could chat to Roger, the crew cox, which made life more amusing. And actually, I thought it made life easier. I didn't have to stay in time with anyone else. I could set a rate and rhythm to suit myself, and the rest of the crew would have to follow me.

Even when the long river so-called 'Head' races started in the springtime, it still didn't bother me. We set off when called into the race, procession style. We might overtake a crew or two and try not to be overtaken. At the end, the times were compared, and the winner determined.

Things changed however in the early summer when the regatta races arrived. These were mostly side by side racing for two crews on twisty river courses. For my very first race at our home course I recall suddenly being short of breath with nerves, while sitting on the start waiting for the 'go' and the accompanying flag drop.

Came the shout and off we went. It was a bit rough and ready but early on we seemed to be in the lead. That wasn't the problem. The problem was the lack of air and the mental pressure in maintaining a rate and rhythm to keep us in the lead. We scraped home ahead, but I was shaken up. Legs were white with weakness, lungs were seriously burning in a way I had never before felt in my life, and my head was spinning. Time to think how to avoid this mess in the future.

I prepared better for the second race. I took some deep breaths (not so much inhaling to fill the lungs, as first exhaling completely to clear the CO_2, as I had been told) and that reduced the air problem. The opposition this time were deemed to be a quick novice crew. I thought maybe we could put the mental pressure on to them.

Off the start and we were down immediately. I focussed on rate, rhythm and breathing, and didn't look. After a couple of minutes the river swung our way and then I saw and heard them. We were overlapping. So they hadn't been able to row away from us. Maybe now we could do something.

Working with Roger in the cox seat, we called a few 'tens' for greater effort, and each time pulled the other boat back a little but at no time did we take the lead. But this was our home course, and I knew well from counting in training just how many strokes were left in the race. When we got to thirty strokes out, I started picking up the rate of strokes per minute, thinking we might go faster. The crew followed me, we seemed to be gaining on the opposition, and so I kept at it. Just in time we came through and passed them, and won by half a length.

And that set the precedent for me in the stroke seat. Let the other crew feel the mental pressure all the way through the race. I really had no choice. I didn't think I could cope with it, so better dump it on to the other fellow. Let him fear that you will come through, but he won't know when. The longer the race, the greater the mental pressure builds. Worse, the leading boat's concentration will move from its own boat to yours, and their technique will suffer for it.

It didn't always work. Sometimes you bumped into a crew from which you just rowed away, and the distance grew as the race went on. They were the easy races. Sometimes a crew just rowed away from you. If that happened, the only tactic was to try to ensure that the rate set would move your own boat at its greatest speed, and if that allowed you to catch the opposition later in the race, and to try to attack them before the finish, then marvellous. If it didn't, then so be it.

The Big Rowing Mistakes

It is of course obvious that the rower uses the oar to move the boat. But it is astonishing how many oarsfolk believe that when they sit in a boat they think of themselves sending the puddle away behind the boat at the end of the stroke. Well I did in any event, for far too long.

The oar is merely a large lever. Once in the water, the oar blade doesn't really move that much. What moves is the boat being levered past the spot where the oar blade sits in the water. If rowers can grasp that, they realise that all the effort should be designed to maximise the leverage to propel the boat past the entry point of the oar.

Which is why I have always wondered about the efficacy of rowing 'tanks', dummy training boats sitting in a tank of water on dry land. There, the oar does move through the water, and it is not possible to lever the pretend boat past the spot. The surrounding concrete tends somewhat to inhibit that possibility.

The most vital thing in rowing, however, is to ensure that when you have levered the boat past the entry point of your oar that you do not negate your effort by rushing up the slide to commence the next stroke. A sudden transfer of your weight will stop the boat in the water between rowing strokes and undo all forward motion, almost regardless of the strength and fitness in the boat. Hence John's oft repeated refrain, 'slow fuckin' down'.

An eight-oared boat with poor weight transfer technique will proceed along in lurches, virtually stopping between strokes. You can readily tell this from a distance by watching the bow ball at the front of the boat. If it stays vertically level as the crew continues to row along, and if in addition the bow doesn't continuously surge and stop horizontally, the chances are that the crew is transferring the weight in a controlled fashion and the boat is moving along nicely.

A crew moving subtly up the slide while the oar is being positioned between strokes will see the boat 'run' between strokes. The difference can be enormous in a race. The sport is not therefore merely about the size of the competitors. Just being a meathead won't do it. Some lightweight crews will be faster than heavier counterparts. Technique, and especially the maintenance of it in a pressurised race environment, is vital in rowing. No fast crew is without it.

Fog, Bog and Water

Later that season, sometime in May, we went off to a regatta somewhere west, out near where I had spent some years in my youth. No one had told them out there that spring had sprung. The day combined freezing cold fog with a drizzle of sleet on top, as they say in the finest recipes. We dutifully rowed to the starting stake boats at the edge of the reeds on the big wide lake, for our first ever six lane race.

Well, there were supposed to be six lanes, but since there were no buoys it was anyone's guess where on the lake the lanes were actually hiding. And in any event, the thick fog precluded any decent visibility. It was actually quite eerie. We sat shivering in our cotton tops and baggy woollen shorts until the starter got around to calling us up for our race.

The regatta was late. It was hours late and the poor old starter chap had been out there all day. He was, however, well equipped with a shotgun which he used to ensure that all crews on the course heard the start at the same time, regardless of the level of sleet or fog. Clever really.

What was not so clever was that he was also well equipped with a bottle of Jameson's Finest Ten Year Old, purely to keep the cold out you will understand. As the day wore on, the level in the bottle declined, as did the elevation of the starting gun. By the time we approached the stake boats, it seemed to me to be aimed directly at Roger, cowering in the cox's seat.

Of course, the next discharge from the declining gun did not actually hit anyone when it went off to mark the start of our race, but what it did do was to disturb a near-by swan who instantly assumed that Roger had caused the deafening roar, and set off to discuss the matter with him. They're pretty large birds all in all, and this fella was big and mean looking and moving fast. He was travelling just above the water as they do, with that unique loud whooshing sound as his giant wings beat up and down. And leading the charge was his orange tipped spear aimed right at us.

Sitting facing Roger in the stroke seat, and more importantly facing the swan, I drew his attention to the encroaching bird. He turned around to see for himself and a millisecond later he was screaming 'Power Ten' at the crew. I was only too happy to raise the rate to levels never before seen in poor old *Hazel*. You see it had quickly occurred to me that once Roger no longer formed a human barrier to this enraged trumpeter, I was next on the swan's Menu du Jour. I had never before thought much about swans, but as the giant wings powered him ever closer, and the rude beak thrust nearer and nearer, I decided this was not the moment either.

We had not quite finished the first count of ten when Roger was already screaming for another and so, demonstrating all the coordination of a demented eggbeater with eight dislocated whisks, we took off down the course, flailing away until the white avenging angel decided we had been warned enough. He faded back into the fog. It was hardly a surprise when we were declared the winners.

'We should bottle that fucker and use him in every race,' said a delighted Kieran as we were presented with unexpectedly decent pewter tankards. It was all right for him. He was somewhere up in the bows, several swan feasts away.

In some ways Year Zero was the best year. We didn't know what we didn't know. We knew we didn't know lots, but we also knew there was time next year to learn more. Meanwhile, we were content just to mill around the place before the rowing, and to do the same afterwards. They were a fun crew, it was a fun club, and being 'the dregs' we had no duties or responsibilities. No pressure.

Boy, was that about to change.

Year One

New York

I returned to Trinity in late September 1974, having spent three months doing menial jobs for a lot of money (in Irish terms) in New York City. My arrival in NYC turned out to be a tad chaotic. I had secured the infamous temporary working J1 visa through the good offices of my father who had procured the required written job offer from the owner of a bar in New York.

That all sounded fine until I walked into the Shamrock Bar in the Bronx and made myself known to the head barman who looked at me carefully before saying

'Bud out sonny. We're not having goddam students in here undercutting our rates.' Well he didn't actually say 'bud out'. He was slightly more rude but I got the message. Great start.

At least my accommodation would be secure as I sought out my father's first cousin in Lower Manhattan. He had let her know when I was coming and had asked her to give me a bed for a few nights until I started work and found my own place. There was no answer at her front door, so I hung around, and around, and around, until it got dark. Being down to my last $20 and assuming that the Waldorf-Astoria might chew up most of that for a night's kip (well, I have warned you I was horribly naive), all I could think of was to head over to the student hostel and book myself in.

The following morning I walked up to Park Avenue (it seemed a nice enough road) and decided I would go into every building and ask for a job. Surely someone would want someone like me. Miraculously, somehow it worked, and the following day I started work as a relief doorman at a sniffy condominium called the Beekman Hotel. Goodness, was that a brush with a new reality. The people who lived there were truly amazing. They probably still are. It's still there so you can go and check for yourself.

One apartment owner was the sister of poor Sharon Tate who was the victim of the crazed Manson killings. Being also the sole heiress to the Folger Coffee fortune, she was understandably very concerned for her security. The precautions taken when she entered and left the building made the President's Secret Service detail look like a bunch of three-year-olds playing Cowboys and Indians. Wall to wall black suits, black limos and from what I could see, black guns in black holsters.

I didn't even have to do my job of opening the door and saying good morning and good evening. I wasn't let anywhere near it, nor her. The first time the security crew saw me, they backed me up against the wall, asked me who the hell I was, called the manager on the house phone to appear and vouch personally for me, and then told me to stand to one side and not move until they had gone. I took them at their word and didn't budge for an hour afterwards. I never did get to see Ms. Folger's face in all the three months I worked there.

Noo Yoik Cops

That first Saturday, I was on duty standing outside the Beekman door admiring Park Avenue as the evening darkened and the lights started to come on. They seemed to stretch all the way up to the sky. It was and remains an astonishing view. I was getting a crick in my neck when a police patrol car pulled up.

Out stepped two large cops. They seemed to me to be drawing their oversized batons as they crossed the pavement towards me. (They were in fact rearranging them on their belts having been obliged to remove them when seated in the car, but I hadn't yet seen enough cop shows on the telly to know this.)

'Wanna tok to you sonny,' said one of them menacingly.

I backed away quickly and very nervously until I banged my head against the front door and could go no further. I thought, 'what on earth have I done now.'

'You gotta Mr. X living here?'

I remembered the name from having sorted the post.

'Yes,' I said in a desperate rush to please them.

'He go out in the mornings, what time?'

I babbled that Mr. X always drove out from the underground car park at about seven each weekday morning and headed downtown.

'You don't say nuthin' to nobody 'bout this, ya hear?'

I nodded. They stared at me for a while to ram the point home. I got it, they left, and I immediately went into the desk manager and blabbed everything.

'Anyone see you tokkin to dem cops?'

I said no.

'Then keep your goddamn mouth shut about this and you might just keep your job.'

I promised, and then told him my favourite police joke. 'Maybe they were looking for a man selling marijuana to birds. They are clearly leaving no tern unstoned.'

He stared blankly at me. 'Why in gawd's name did we ever give you a job?'

To tell you the truth, I was beginning to wonder myself. Time to get back to my door.

Turned out the police arrested Mr. X as he left the car park on Monday morning. A Wall Street titan apparently, on some mammoth fiddle. Weren't they all? Why pick on him? I didn't ask and wasn't told.

Fired and Fried

There was a staff rumpus one afternoon as I showed up for work. One of the other men coming on at the same time showed up seriously drunk, and the manager fired him on the spot. They had to call security to show him the door.

The following week I was on the night shift and towards the morning, as the building and surrounding streets were waking up, I took a look outside just as it was getting light at around 6.00 am. There was thick fog making visibility impossible.

The first apartment owner of the day emerged from the elevator and headed for the front door. As I began to open it, he stopped and said, 'what's burning?'

I said, 'it's only fog.'

'In August in Manhattan?' looking at me in disbelief, and to be fair, I thought he might have had a point. Just at that moment there was an enormous bang. The force of it slammed the front door wide open against my face and whacked me on to the floor. I was going off that door. We just weren't operating as a team.

What now, I thought, counting legs and arms and quickly getting to four which I thought was about right. The sirens began their yowling, the blue lights appeared, and chaos reigned outside the front door for the next half hour with all the uniforms standing around looking tough but not, it seemed, actually doing anything.

The manager then appeared and quickly got the facts with which he reassured the various owners who had assembled in the lobby. It transpired that some nutter had lit a fire under a car parked further down Park Avenue, and after a little time the fuel tank had gone up.

'Odd thing to do,' mused the manager. We all agreed.

When the fuss died down and the smoke had cleared, we went out to have a look. It was then he realised that the barbequed car was his. It turned out that the recent former employee had objected to being fired and had returned to even things up a tad. Since then, the phrase 'getting fired' has always carried an additional meaning for me.

The Difference between Black and Blue

The Attorney General of New York lived in the building. Every morning, five days a week, promptly at 8.00 am, the longest black car I had ever seen would pull up outside the front door. I would telephone up, and a few moments later Mr. Louis J. Lefkowitz would appear, bid me a genial good morning, and cross the pavement to where the chauffeur would be holding open the car door. Off he went, to return late most evenings.

One morning a battered blue sedan appeared at the allotted time. I was suspicious until I saw the usual chauffeur emerge, and so I made the usual call, and off went Louis. When the same car appeared every day that week, I summoned up the courage to ask the great man what had happened to his magnificent black charabanc.

'Election time,' he said with a big grin, 'gotta look like I'm a man of the people when I go round the boroughs.' He got re-elected and the black limo was back the next morning. Welcome to politics in the US of A.

I think I learnt more about life standing by the door of the Beekman Hotel than I had in four years of expensive boarding school. I was never sure whether any of it might be relevant to later life though. In some ways I guess I was hoping none of it.

Ali

The job finished for me when all the regular doormen and receptionists had taken their summer breaks. I still had some time, however, before my return flight and so I went walking again looking for a few more weeks of work. The doorman money was good even if the work was hideously boring when not occasionally enlivened, so I tried alternative buildings. I got lucky in a building on West 59th Street (Central Park South) and with it came my biggest claim to fame.

Late one evening, I was working the night shift at reception when there was a kerfuffle outside. A crowd gathered, a few cars drew up and from the lead car out stepped Muhammad Ali with an entourage of a half dozen people. Flashlights went off, the crowd surged and the yelling and whoopin' started. It was all very good natured and from what I could see the big man was enjoying the banter.

And then all of a sudden he was through the doors and into my reception. I gaped at him. He was truly an enormous fellow with a huge presence. The bonhomie had vaporised however and somewhat sternly he looked at me and said, 'any mail?' Holy cow, he lived where I worked.

I looked through the pile and stammered out a 'no' and then suddenly thought as he was turning away if I don't get his autograph no one will ever believe me. So I thrust my book at him and this time stammered out 'autograph' or something garbled along that line. He took the book, scrawled his name, and then out of curiosity turned it over to look at the title. It was Graham Green's *The Comedians*.

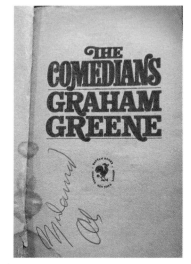

Signature of The Greatest on my coffee-stained book

The big fella looked hard at me.

'You some kinda wise guy?'

I went weak with terror. And then he smiled, returned the book, and I felt the sun shine again, even if it was midnight. I never saw him again during my stay, but I haven't washed the book since either.

But there was only so much real learning I could stand, so as September rolled around I headed off to the airport, Lakered my way to London, and gradually made my way back to the now familiar campus.

It didn't seem quite so forbidding second time round.

Social 'History'

Until the 1970s, the Roman Catholic Church forbade their flock from attending Trinity College. The ban was imposed because the Church considered that attendance at Trinity (originally founded as a Protestant establishment) 'constituted a moral danger to the faith of Irish Catholics', to quote an article from the *New York Times* on June 28, 1970.

Most of us felt the reality was quite different however. We all knew it was to ensure that good Catholic boys would not to be perverted by those immoral Protestant girls. As it turned out over time, the perverts turned out to be a tad closer to home for our esteemed church. And actually the Protestant girls turned out to very interesting indeed to those of us who had never seen them previously, in real life that is. Of course, we'd all seen their pictures in the smuggled magazines. They couldn't have been Catholics. Could they?

One consequence however of this strategic policy was that until the ban was removed, the preponderance of undergraduates attending Trinity stemmed from the Protestant community living on both sides of the Irish border, as well as students from elsewhere in the United Kingdom, and of course further overseas. There were a few Catholics at the university prepared to risk the fires of Hades for all eternity, but they were a small minority.

Unsurprisingly, the Boat Club reflected this general demographic, but it went further than that. A significant proportion of good schools in Northern Ireland had rowing facilities, and hence there had long been a stream of good schoolboy oars joining the Boat Club on arrival at Trinity. Naturally enough, knowing about rowing, they regularly occupied many if not most of the Club's committee posts, and were responsible for the smooth running of its operations.

When the ban was eventually removed, the number of Catholic students from Ireland started rising steadily. By 1973, when my 'generation' arrived, the preponderance of those joining the Boat Club were Katliks from the 'Free State'.

To be polite to us, we were probably cast more in the role of players than gentlemen (and some would say we have not since changed), whereas until then the club members were invariably gentlemen, and more often than not reasonably successful rowing players as well.

There were a few notable exceptions, but in the main, those of us arriving into the Boat Club in the 1970s knew as much about rowing as the average skunk knows about deodorant. Nonetheless, the club was changing in line with the university, and indeed with Irish society more generally, and now of course Trinity has Roman Catholic chaplains to add to their Protestant equivalents.

In truth, this change in make-up of the club membership saw little friction, remarkably so given the awful events unfolding in parallel north of the border from 1969 onwards. If anything, the unity between all those young men from culturally different, yet geographically close, backgrounds confirmed the view that the Troubles in the north of the island lay at the door of extremists with no regard for society, and was not present in the makeup of the overwhelming majority of everyone else resident on that little green, white and orange isle.

In other words, those who came before us were, almost without exception, proper people, exemplified by the aforementioned Tom Noble. But change was afoot and, as the author Raymond Blake elegantly put it in his comprehensive history of the Boat Club *In Black and White*, blue denim was replacing cream flannels.

Despite this innate decency emanating from our forebears, for some of us new 'players' we nonetheless detected a slight feeling that we were making rather more noise than befitted our utter lack of rowing achievements to date. And that was quite true. But as it turned out, it was probably one of the best cultural changes that ever unfolded at the club.

It was nothing to do with backgrounds. We new arrivals got the feeling that we needed to deliver rowing performances to justify our noise level. That feeling gradually translated into pressure to deliver results, as the subsequent years unfolded.

The Big Mac

A new captain had taken over in the Boat Club. Donagh J. McDonagh was a 'mature' student (well, in years anyway) and a true force of nature. He was nearly 30 for goodness sakes. How old can you get? Previous careers in the Irish Army (where he been sent to the US to train with those crazies they call 'Rangers'), and subsequently the Irish Air Force where he flew fast jets (presumably as there were no slow ones available, even to the Irish Defence Forces).

Altogether this meant he was rather more 'experienced', especially with the ladies, than the rest of us put together. Or so he told us maidens, and we looked at him with a mixture of awe and disbelief. We never knew whether he was exaggerating and were quite terrified at the thought that he might not be.

More relevantly, however, and most probably due to his time served at upper altitudes, he immediately set the Boat Club's sights far higher than had been the case for many of the previous decades.

In 1875, Trinity Dublin (as Henley Royal Regatta always refers to it, rightly to distinguish it from replicas with similar names) had won the Ladies Plate at the annual Regatta. This event was initially only for British college crews of eight men (including Trinity), but in later years it had been widened to include universities from around the world.

Despite years of trying, Trinity had not won it since. Notwithstanding that he had rowed only for a couple of years previously, and despite never having been to

Henley, Big Mac decided that winning the Ladies Plate was to be the target, and he would commence the campaign by entering a crew exactly 100 years after the previous victory.

Naturally, when word of this drivel trickled down to our level, we all assumed he was taking the piss. We knew nothing about any Ladies Plates (supposedly so called as the wives of the Stewards who run the Regatta first presented it in 1845, or so I read last night in Wikipedia so it must be true). Worse still, we knew nothing about a Royal Henley, and what was wrong with Shanagarry Regatta in any event? More class there than you could shake a blackthorn stick at.

D.U.B.C. SENIOR VIII 1875.
WINNERS OF THE LADIES' PLATE, HENLEY.

The 1875 Ladies Plate Winning Crew (well, an update)

*From left, Bartholomew (Batty) Reilly, Monroe (Munch) Murnane,
Horatio (Hopeless) Hickey, Sylvester (Squire) Sanfey,
Godfrey (Mighty) McGee, Mortimer (Marty) Mulcahy,
Moncrieff (Monty) Macken, Wilberforce (Willie) Weale
and Melvin (Young Mel) O'Morchoe*

Moreover, the last time we looked, we weren't ladies and why do all this training for a mere plate competition? It made no sense, but it was a Big Mac edict, so as usual we shut up and went all Light Brigade.

Apart from ignorant oarsmen, Big Mac faced a few other hurdles. Trinity crews hadn't really featured at a serious level at Henley for some time; the equipment then available to the rowing squads was old; there was a dearth of experienced coaches; and there was no money to remedy any of these fatal flaws. So when you think about it, a hundred years mostly spent in the Ladies wilderness was not that surprising.

Big Mac didn't see any of those obstacles as insurmountable. This was a man who, as we were beginning to learn, when blocked by whining words and lack of action simply dropped down a gear in his bulldozer and pressed harder on the pedal. You might indeed say that he replaced negative talk with positive torque. He might have left the Army, but the Army hadn't left him. He started marching.

Action Stations

His was a very simple plan, as the best ones always are. Refurbish the Boat House to attract evening parties, generate cash from same and buy new boats and oars with the cash. Appoint people responsible for the parties, the cash and the boat purchases, and drive everyone forward on their tasks. Hup, two, three, four.

Coaching and training regimes, however, were the next big issues. The existing part time training and coaching set up was outdated and, with the very occasional exception, the club had not seen winning crews for quite some years.

It was then that the Big Mac alighted on one Robin Tamplin. Of all his steps taken to update and upgrade the club, the most strategic and successful was the persuasion and subsequent appointment of Robin to become head coach and oversee crew training.

R.W.R. Tamplin Arrives ...

An extraordinarily modest man given the astonishing successes in his life, Robin arrived and commenced the moulding of the club into his image. In his amateur rowing days he had represented Ireland in the 1948 London Olympics, the rowing events for which, as it happened, were raced on the Henley reach of the Thames. Leading an exceptional Trinity crew in 1950, he had reached the final of the Ladies Plate, sadly missing by a few feet what would have been a deserving win.

Professionally, while in the British overseas service, he oversaw the arrival of Idi Amin as President of Uganda, and reputedly held the Union Jack as it was lowered for the last time in that country. Returning to Dublin, he took over the training division of the Guinness Brewery in Dublin, where they used to say he was the only man who knew how to run the entire brewery.

During those latter years he was also responsible for rescuing a drowning man from the freezing and high walled River Liffey, without mentioning a word of it to anybody. It took until his sad funeral some years back for most of his friends and acquaintances to find out about his heroic feat.

Although reports surfaced later that the Brewery had been forced to open both double doors (usually reserved solely for entry and egress of the giant tanker trucks) to allow him to make an unfettered exit following a very fine lunch with Robin, the Big Mac had accomplished his strategic objective. Robin agreed to become head coach on a completely unpaid basis with immediate effect and agreed that the ultimate target was to take the Ladies Plate once again.

Convinced by the Big Mac that the fleet of boats would be upgraded and that there was a sufficiently deep pool of prospectively decent oarsmen, Robin agreed to return to the club to assess for himself the calibre of the squads then present. He paid little attention to the denim, jeans, noise and haircuts. Probably just as well in the case of the haircuts. Or rather, lack thereof. He knew that all that lay on the surface.

What he was after lay deeper in men, and with his background he knew how to determine what motivated any one individual. It transpired afterwards that he was searching for commitment. He knew from first-hand experience what sacrifices would be required to get anywhere close to the ambition first voiced by Big Mac. He also knew that as head coach he would have to make sacrifices in his own life, and he needed to be sure it would be worthwhile.

Moreover, Robin also knew, which we did not, that international rowing had become seriously competitive, and unofficially professional, with much attention being devoted to the science of the sport. It wasn't just that boats and oars were using new materials. The nature and degrees of training being practiced by the top crews around the world meant that the Boat Club had some serious catching up to do.

... And Assembles His Gang of Four

Robin knew how to oversee rowing, but still recognised that there would be a need to draft in a circle of other coaches, each delivering different things.

So Rob Van Mesdag was sent for. Another former Trinity man and a Dutch international in his younger days, he had remained the superb single sculler which he had always been, and by virtue of being a London-based reporter he had his ear very close to the developments in international rowing.

Nick Tinne appeared. A former Oxford Blue, following a tradition in that regard set by both his father and grandfather, Nick understood precisely what moved a boat. Being quietly spoken he surprised us initially, but we quickly learnt to listen to his accurate summary of the good and bad aspects of any outing he oversaw.

Chris George What?

And then finally a chap called Chris George arrived. He didn't appear to have a proper surname. We were told merely that he was from England, that he had raced for Trinity in the ancient past, that he was currently rowing with the GB Lightweight squad (so actually not that ancient), and that he would graciously observe for a few outings to assess whether we were of any use before returning to his London berth. He was actually an outstanding oarsman and had the pedigree to prove it. He was lightweight rowing World Champion for GB in the mid-1970s while simultaneously amassing a decent collection of Henley winning medals in various different crews and various different events. Just don't get him started on a discussion about technique, however, if you have plans for the weekend ...

Great, we thought. Last thing we needed was an English know-all 'expert' at the top of the rowing tree come to tell us how crap we were. We already knew that.

He arrived at Islandbridge early one Saturday and we paid him not the slightest notice. By this time I was in the stroke seat of the first VIII as Robin chopped and changed us trying to figure out the fastest combination. I wasn't altogether convinced I had the mental strength or experience to lead a senior crew to Shanagarry, let alone lead an outright win at Henley, but Robin knew what he was doing and so I wasn't overly concerned. As long as I was somewhere in the boat, I would be content.

That Saturday we rowed the mile or so upriver to the turning point, Robin and Chris following on their bikes. We spun the boat, came back down and were told to go to the launching slip. We did so and Chris ambled over as we sat there looking up at him, curious as to what was going on.

Pointing at me he said, 'I want you out of there mate.'

I'm not your mate, I said to myself, but obediently got out and walked up to the Boat House. Great. The expert know-all had dropped me out of the boat. Stuff it, I thought. The boatman's dog wisely having sized up the situation and faded from view, I kicked the wall all the way into the Boat House.

Thinking more sensibly, I realised that if I went back immediately to my rooms, I could shower, drop off my kit, get the bus into An Lar and take the train to Longford in time to see my parents for the rest of the weekend. I enjoyed spending time with them, but I didn't much enjoy trying to figure out over the entire weekend what else I might do apart from rowing.

I returned to the college on Monday night, and on Tuesday morning between lectures I dropped into the

Boat Club rooms, wondering whether there might be a half decent second crew to be formed in which I could continue rowing.

'Where the fuck have you been?' was the greeting. I looked my usual blank self.

'We couldn't row without you, there was no spare man.'

Oops.

Years later, by which time I had come to regard Chris as a good friend (it might even be mutual by now, his memory is fading…), I finally got around to asking him what he had hoped to achieve that morning by dropping me. Having studied at Trinity a decade previously, he knew exactly the reception in store for him from a bunch of surly Irishmen and decided that the only way he could be taken seriously would be to make an early change in the crew. That would get our attention.

His plan, however, was to swap me into a different seat and to allow someone else to stroke the boat for a while. I hadn't picked up on that subtlety and inadvertently buggered up his entire strategy. An unintended collapse of one strategic plan, and a big lesson to me to listen more carefully in life.

At Swim, No Birds (with apologies to Flann O'Brien)

I was living in Trinity Hall, comfortable student accommodation in a posh part of Dublin's southern 'burbs. It was mixed, but boys and girls were in different buildings, hence the proper name was 'Virginity Hall'. It was an awful moniker since we boys were all terrified that we could end up leaving university and still be virgins. The other problem with it, however, was that it was some five miles from the Boat House and that meant a long cycle to and from every outing.

In January 1975, the Boat Club was enjoying a flood of fresh entrants in addition to those like myself who had returned from the previous year. One such was Mark, a decent, well-bred English fellow who had learned his rowing at Eton or Radley, or one of those nice English schools where sons of the gentry were taught how to rule over the peasants of Ireland. Or so I decided. Mark was billeted at the Hall and had a car, a Ford Escort estate. They were an unusual build in that they had three, not five, doors, including the boot. You will see in a moment why this is important to remember.

That month the weather got really nasty, with snow and ice and bitterly low temperatures, especially in the dark mornings. One Friday night, Mark very kindly offered the cox, Roger White, and me a lift to the Boat House on the Saturday morning for the planned outing. It took us about a nanosecond to accept. I didn't really mind being a trodden-on peasant if I could be warm.

The latter half of the route from the Hall to the Boat House is along the Grand Canal. It was, and remains, an attractive part of Dublin. One side of the canal runs along parallel to the road, and at the other side next to the pavement there is a one foot high parapet wall. On the other side of this wall the grass slope slips smoothly down to the water.

The treacherous Grand Canal in winter.

Early that morning, as the sun was coming up, we set off for our rowing outing. The road was a beautiful straight line of unbroken white, untouched snow. The ice lay hidden beneath.

I was chatting to Mark from the passenger seat and Roger was dozing in the rear. I was clearly boring Mark rigid as from time to time he waggled the steering wheel, waited for the tail of the car to come around, and then immediately twirled the steering wheel the other way until the car straightened up. It was quite a long straight road and Mark's ambition rose with his confidence, and soon we were moving along quite smartly, with Mark exhibiting greater and greater mastery of the conditions. Until he wasn't.

The tail of the car came around and Mark's steering twirl had no effect. At a fairly decent speed the rear wheels of the car hit the pavement which bounced its tail up onto the one foot parapet, and then with a terrible screeching noise the car tore itself over the parapet and slid backwards down the grassy slope and into the water.

It all happened in fast motion. One moment I was sitting warm and comfortable, and it seemed only a second later that the water was rising rapidly through the cabin of the car. It was shockingly cold. It was so cold I scarcely registered that it was also wet.

The canal is not overly deep and so the car came to rest with its front bumper just sticking out of the water and touching the bank. The boot lid was sitting happily on the bottom of the canal. The cabin though was completely under water and, it seemed, instantly full of the stuff. I couldn't get the door open, but dimly remembering some lifeguard training undertaken years before (or maybe I saw it on *Baywatch*), I quickly wound down the window. I don't know whether Lekky windows had been invented by then, but fortunately Fords didn't seem to have them. I could sense that the car wasn't sinking further, and so I implicitly assumed that we would get out, but then I suddenly remembered Roger. No rear doors. Not good.

As I was turning around to look for him I got a bang on the head and concluded that Roger was en route. Time to get out. I slithered out through the window as fast as I could with Roger hard on my heels. We surfaced immediately, took a stroke or two, reached out, and clawed our way up the grassy bank to the parapet. We sat there cold and confused, panting with adrenaline and fear, looking back at the canal. And as we sat and stared, we saw the car quietly and gently roll over to one side and disappear completely from view. That started the shivering, big time.

Mark was already seated on the parapet.

'If anyone asks' he said, 'the story is that there was black ice and there was nothing I could do.'

I thought, if anyone asks I'll tell them he's a fucking fruitcake.

But he did look very cool. I was thinking that they really did have something going for them, these Eton or Radley boys. Until, that was, I saw him trying to light a damp flaccid cigarette with the water leaking out of his lighter. Posh fucking fruitcake.

What the hell to do now? We stood, drenched, frozen and looking around. It was eight in the morning. All decent Christians were tucked up in bed, no buses ran down that route at that hour on a Saturday, and mobile phones were still awaiting the birth of Mr. Nokia. We were in our rowing kit, and our dry clothes were now ten feet under and no doubt a tad damp. Hypothermia here we come. Nothing for it but to run to the Boat House and huddle by the boiler until we dried out.

After about twenty minutes we got there, soaked, shivering and gasping. We thought we had done well but recognised that we were a tad late on parade. There were about thirty oarsmen of varying status milling around the boating slip. It was then that Big Mac spotted us.

'You Trinity Hall lot, upstairs in the Long Room now.'

We trudged and dripped up the stairs to the Long Room, awaiting his sympathy and support.

'Youze are dropped,' said Big Mac, 'so yez can feck off now. No rowing for ye.'

I stood gaping at him.

'What are ya lookin' at?' he growled at me.

Now Big Mac was not a man with whom to tangle. We well understood from his background that he knew how to command men, and miserable little undergraduates didn't feature on his Richter scale of them.

To a nervous 19-year-old, he was an awesome personality and usually in the few dealings I had with him, I had always felt that melting back to blend into the undergrowth was the best strategy for continuing to enjoy my short life with limbs still attached. But this time I really was indignant.

'But we've been in a car accident,' I stammered.

'The road was icy, and the car went into the canal,' said Roger supportively.

'We were lucky to get out with our lives,' I stuttered on, trying to convey the reality of the story, and then stopped, daring to look up at him.

He held my gaze and, looking contemptuously, said, 'do you honestly expect me to believe a word of that shite? Now feck off.'

I guess they didn't do prisoners in his army. And as for sympathy, the message was clear. It can be found in the dictionary between shit and syphilis. He didn't even need to say it.

I have no memory of getting back to Virginity Hall that morning, but I do recall cycling every weekend thereafter. And bugger the weather.

In the Water, Again

Some ten years later I had another brush with unexpected swimming.

'Are you fit and free this weekend?' asked the voice on my phone, ten years after I had last held an oar in anger.

'Reasonably and yes,' I said.

'Well there's a flight to Pisa on Friday evening, take the train to Viareggio and we'll meet you there. You'll be racing in an VIII on Saturday morning made up from a couple of Trinity blokes and the rest from UCD. It's the World Veteran Rowing Champs, and this crew is quick.'

No hesitation at my end.

Viareggio on Saturday morning was glorious, as was the lake close to where Puccini spent a part of his life, and where there is still an annual opera festival held in his honour. Surrounded by big white marble bearing mountains, but with enough forests and woodlands to keep it looking wild and woolly, it was a beautiful rowing location. And all the better for the settled weather that morning. Settled? Was it hell.

I clambered into the 4 seat of the VIII and the crew set off for the race. No time for a long practice run, but it was not needed as the rest had been rowing together all year. One back injury the previous weekend, and I had got the call to substitute. The start was rehearsed with me, we practiced with a few quick tens and a twenty, and then lined up on the stake boat. The names of the countries represented by the six crews were called out on the Tannoy with our boat 'Irlanda' somewhere in the middle. It was all happening so quickly I didn't have time to work up my usual stress and panic at the start of a race.

'*Et Vous Pret? Partez!*' and the boat took off. In those days, all international races were started in French. I really don't know why. Sounded more upmarket I guess.

One of the most cultivated oars ever to grace UCD crews, Jay Renehan, was in the stroke seat. He was one of the very few tall men who seemed able to combine stroke length, searing speed through the water, and a boat moving rhythm. For once I was enjoying a race from the very beginning. It felt fast but easy, long but quick, and unsurprisingly we got our noses in front and steadily drew out a lead of a boat length. We came into the finish nicely ahead and turned immediately to the landing slip to collect our medals. World Champions in our age group at 11 o'clock in the morning sounded good to me, and somewhat elated, we happy band of men headed immediately off to the bar. Work for the weekend all done. Or so I thought.

The UCD boys had also entered a coxless four and so they went off in a huddle while the rest of us finished our first pints of Heineken and prepared to settle in for the remainder of the gallon while watching the rest of the races from the comfort of the bar overlooking the course. I was halfway through my second pint when Jay and two more of the four loomed large over me.

'Put that down. We need you again.'

'What?'

'There's been a disagreement, and someone's walked off. Will you race the coxless IV with us?'

The Heineken in me answered definitely not, but off I went anyway.

The yellow Empacher boat to which I was directed had low sides but was known to be light and quick. I settled into the bow seat at the sharp end, Jay again was at stroke in the stern and with Big Jim Skelly and his mate in the middle, I was satisfied it would be a quick combination.

I hadn't really noticed it while in the bar, but the sunlight had faded, clouds had built up and a wind had appeared. As we headed to the start it continued to freshen and by the time we reached the start it was shockingly strong and coming right across the course. Waves had got up and the umpire was clearly struggling to marshal crews into straight lines before starting the races. Every time he had three or four more or less in line, three or two would be broadside on to the course and incapable of racing away.

We sat quietly observing the growing confusion and as time dragged on it became obvious that the starts were becoming more and more chaotic. By now the regatta was running at least an hour late and getting later by the minute. Where was Il Duce when rowing needed him?

It was Jim sitting in front of me who first spotted that by now the races were being started even if only a bare majority of the six crews were in line.

'Lads, when we're on the stake boat, we need to get the effing thing angled into the wind, and at the last minute I'll take a stroke to straighten her. And we are going on the *Pret* not the *Partez*. In these conditions they won't even be able to tell if we jump it, never mind calling us back.'

He might have been big, and he might have been the world champion in the annual indoor rowing events, which he was for years, but he was even smarter than he was big. And he was very big. I figured he was pushing maybe seventeen stone of pure muscle and technique.

We came on to the starting stakeboats and tried to line up. As soon as we heard the *Et* Jim took half a stroke. To our intense relief, the boat came round beautifully and we were gone as the *Pret* came over the Tannoy, to be instantly whipped away by the wind. As it turned out, the starter's voice wasn't the last thing that day to be whipped away by the wind.

We were in lane one, first in line for the breeze, and were powering away sharpish, comfortably in the lead from three or four other boats. So far, so good. It didn't last. The waves were getting higher and higher, and water was now slopping noticeably over the sides of the boat. Simultaneously, I realised we had crossed into the adjacent lane but then every other boat had also been shoved across the course.

As the race went on the wind picked up and soon it was howling and shrieking viciously down the valley between the mountains and across the lake. The noise was by now truly astonishing and the waves were piling up higher and higher. It was a shockingly sudden transformation.

We're not going to make this, I thought to myself, but we rowed on, crashing and banging the oars in and out as much as the conditions allowed. Sometimes I would get a good clean stroke, sometimes the wave would hit the oar on the recovery phase, and I could not move it up the boat in time to match the next stroke. But still we struggled on.

Meanwhile, the severity of the wind was continuing to force each boat further and further across the course. Passing the halfway mark, I realised one crew was already in the water off to my left, with a safety launch powering across towards the swimming oarsmen. In our boat the water was now sloshing over my rowing shoes and the overall level was rising alarmingly. What to do?

I watched the waves rising higher and higher and then someone screamed out, 'power down, power down, sit on the wave, sit on the wave. It will carry us.' We all caught on, Jay dropped the rate, and we started surfing. We didn't get it entirely right, from time to time slipping off the wave and seeing the next one wash down towards the boat, but we were still afloat. Just.

For us it now became less of a race against the other crews and simply a race to get as close to the finish as we could before the inevitable sinking. It was clearly coming and when it did, it was sudden. We slid off a wave and its immediate follower simply rolled over the entire boat, submerging us up to our waists and bringing the boat to an immediate stop. Game over.

Now as we know a racing shell won't usually sink if it remains whole, as the outstretched oars will provide sufficient buoyancy. The biggest danger is if the middle of the boat fills with water while the long sealed buoyancy spaces at the bow and stern remain full of air. Should that happen boats can split in the middle and be utterly destroyed.

Rowers in sinking boats are therefore schooled in two critical actions. Get your feet out of the screwed in rowing shoes immediately, and if you are the cox or the bow man, open the covered areas at either end to allow some water in to avoid a split.

Back in Viareggio, I got the cover to the bow space open but was fighting hard to get my feet out of the shoes. They finally burst free and I slid my feet towards me and under the oar and then I slipped fully into the water, joining my crew mates. Being July, thankfully it was warm and so I wasn't seriously concerned. I grabbed my oar which was still locked on to the boat via the retaining rigger, and hung on catching my breath. It was still all a bit surreal, however; I had left the bar for this?

By now the Heineken had fully worn off, and as I was also getting my face washed every few seconds, things generally weren't amusing me much. Clearly the lake was taking its revenge for our cheek of having sat on its waves. I looked around to see where we were and realised that we had in fact passed the finish line, but having started out in lane one, we were now submerged in lane six. As far as I could tell from a brief watery glance around, the other boats and crews were also all under water.

It seemed an age before we were towed to the shore, which was thankfully not that far away and, having struggled up the beach, we realised that the boat was undamaged, and so we were able to empty it out, refloat it, attach the oars, and climb back in. As we were heading gingerly towards the landing slip, the organisers showed their appreciation by determining that we had actually finished the race in first place, and so a second 'World Veteran Rowing Champion' medal was hung around our necks. It was doubly welcome, and meant I could renew my acquaintance with Heineken with even greater satisfaction.

And all of that happened within an hour. It felt like a lifetime.

Time Out

But back to 1975. Big Mac was still in charge. Strange as it may seem after the canal incident, he and I subsequently became very good friends.

Years later, when I was working in London as an investment banker (with a 'b' was Mac's regular little joke), I had to do what all bankers had to do in the 1980s, and that was to buy a Porsche. I knew we both shared a love of all things motoring and so I proposed to him that we might give the car a run back whence it came, namely Stuttgart. He jumped at the chance, and off we went.

It was January, it was a dark Friday night, and Stuttgart had feet of snow everywhere we looked. Stuck in heavy traffic, Mac spotted a narrow road off to our left heading in the general direction of our hotel.

'You're a navigational genius, Mac,' I said and swung the wheel.

The road was narrow and banked up with snow on both sides. Not a single car. How smart were we. I rounded a corner at a legal 30 kilometres per hour and saw a car with a single headlamp coming towards us.

'Very un-Germanic,' said Mac. I agreed. It came closer. Also very un-carlike. It wasn't a car. It was the sodding tram and it took up the entirety of the 'road' from snowbank to snowbank. Oh, and it was barrelling along nicely as it hit the bell, klaxon and loud indignant horn simultaneously. With a sudden feeling of dread we realised that it was obviously not planning to stop and for all the world I thought we were about to get seriously Blitzkrieged. We were sitting ducks.

Now the Porsche was one of the cheaper ones, having only a canvas roof rather than the full metal jacket. That meant there was a small slit where the rear glass window would normally sit. Finding reverse gear was easy. Actually seeing out the back while reversing the car away from the charging metal monster bearing down on us still gives me nightmares. The damn tram was getting closer and closer and I could see the driver now towering over us. I swear he was grinning lasciviously at the thought of the fun coming his way. Playing squash with the little Englanders (as he thought). What better entertainment could a German tram driver dream of?

I don't know how we got back but somehow we shot back out tail first on to the main road, swivelled around, and re-joined the queue of traffic without hitting anything. Mac said the tram driver's face showed serious disappointment as the tracks bore him off the other direction. I didn't doubt it.

You'd think we'd learn.

Two days later heading to an unfamiliar boutique hotel in the hills outside the city for our last night, we were again surrounded by the snow, but this time we were deep in the dark countryside and without a detailed map. Didn't matter. Mac had all the navigational experience in the world, including some from being high in the sky. I didn't need to worry. Yeah, right.

We both spotted the hotel name on a signpost, and with relief I turned down the laneway and into an enormous, but oddly empty, car park. As we crept along the snow covered surface wondering where the other guest cars were, we passed a wooden structure jutting out from the side.

'For collecting milk churns,' I said confidently.

'This is clearly a big milk producing area,' continuing to dig a crater for myself.

'Mmmm,' said Mac. 'Looks to me like a jetty.'

'Why would they have a jetty in a car park?' As I said it, the answer hit me.

I froze. Mac froze.

'You don't think...' Yup, the lake had frozen too, sometime earlier.

We got the name of the place correct, but we had missed the little word 'See' on the signpost. We were on the lake which was overlooked by the hotel. I suddenly understood all those war films when the soldiers had to step carefully through the minefields. Again, I reversed for our lives, but this time infinitesimally slowly with Mac hanging out his door looking backwards as he guided me, desperately trying to follow our tracks exactly until we hit the reassuring bump of the lake shore.

When we got to the actual car park of the hotel, which did have other guest cars parked there, we were not surprised to see the hotel entrance crowded by their owners. They had probably sold tickets. What on earth were those madmen doing driving around on the frozen lake? They did give us a drink on the house, but it was definitely not worth it.

We had one last adventure on that mad trip. We crossed Belgium at high speed from the German autobahn and only a few minutes later (it seemed) we hit France. The autoroute was three lanes wide and completely empty.

The Porsche was deep into three figures (and I'm not talking 911) when we crested a small hill and straight ahead, just beyond a motorway entrance ramp, sat two Gendarmerie cars, lights flashing, sirens wailing and a couple of heavily armed boys in blue gesticulating violently at us. The whole nine yards laid out just for us. Mac said afterwards that he had spied a helicopter a short time previously but hadn't done the resulting maths in time.

I braked, pulled over just after the entrance ramp, and stopped.

'Monsieur, you drive too fast,' came the snarl from the moustachioed Gendarme as he reached for *la plume de ma tante*, and what I knew would be a very expensive piece of *papier*.

It was at that moment she blasted past down the autoroute entrance ramp. A blond, sitting behind a pair of dark glasses. That would normally have attracted some attention, but on this occasion the attention score went sky high. She was driving an open top orange Lamborghini and it howled past us all as she went up the gears.

Well, forget a few lads in a Porsche. This was far more fun. Les Flics ran for both cars and powered after her. Mac and I sat there stunned.

After a few minutes he said, 'parking by a motorway is not a safe thing to do. We ought to go somewhere a bit safer.'

'Like London?' I said.

'Exactly.'

We did and it was. Never heard another squeak.

Fortunately, no photographs exist of the trip to Stuttgart, but just to prove the friendship, here is a photograph taken a few stones later, when the pair were driving the author's 1939 Bentley in the Mallorcan mountains. It was a safer trip, there being no snow, trams or indignant Gendarmes.

Nottingham, Bloody Nottingham

Towards the end of that racing season, Robin reckoned that we needed more racing experience and so he entered us to race the week before Henley at the Nottingham International Regatta. We arrived on the Friday and looked around us. Of course, we had seen six lane rowing courses before. We had even seen them with the occasional buoys anchored near the start or the finish (rarely both). But this was something truly in a different league.

A purpose-built facility, with every lane buoyed and stretching away into the dim distance for the full 2000 metres. With cabins marking each 500 metre mark, fixed starting rafts, and even race photography at the finish for goodness sake, this was a different rowing world. There were mobile grandstands towed by tractors which meant for the first time in our experience, it was possible for spectators to follow every race from directly alongside. It was professional, well thought out and well built, and utterly impersonal. In truth, it was more than a little intimidating.

The intimidation grew when we realised that since the annual World Rowing Championships were taking place there later that year, all the world's top international crews had appeared to test out the facility. We hadn't seen Russian and Bulgarian national crews before, but most of all, we had never encountered the infamous East Germans. At the height of their state-sponsored rowing prowess, they had a fearsome reputation for consistent winning. Giants were suddenly stalking our little rowing earth.

That first evening, when we had finished our practice runs and subsequently showered and changed, we went out on to the terrace of the grandstand to look again at the course.

It was then we saw him. Right at the forward end of the balcony railings and facing down the course to the start, he was sitting hunched over. By his size we assumed that he was or had been a cox. We then noticed the most enormous set of binoculars resting on a tripod. Never mind viewing the stars, they were long enough to touch them. Gazing though the lenses, he was studying what seemed to be a crew in the far distance.

We edged closer. He had a bag on the floor. It was emblazoned with the Stars and Stripes. Coach of the

American crews we surmised. He was muttering away to himself as he studied the crew.

'Look Dave, another nutter,' said Rory.

'I don't agree,' said the observant John. 'Look at his ears.'

I was thinking Star Trek Spock and wondered what John was on about. Staring at the ears, we first noticed the black hearing aids, and then we saw the matching black microphone. What on earth?

It took a while but we worked it out. He was only bloody coaching his crew from two kilometres away. And doing it by talking quietly to the cox. While we were still using bicycles and loud hailers. We were stunned into silence.

Kieran voiced it for us all as we walked away.

'Looks like they've only gone and got the fucking CIA helping with their training. Jesus, what chance have we?'

On the Saturday we raced the level below the international lot and won the VIII's event. That meant automatically having to race at the higher international level on Sunday, but sadly Nottingham's infamous and capricious weather arrived to make the course unrowable, and so we never got the chance to whip the Easties. As if.

Two of us did make initial contact with some of the East German men's VIII by the Boat House, but we were quickly spotted by the goon squad. As they were prohibited from making contact with degenerate Westerners, we were quickly shooed away and they were all quickly marshalled off to their waiting bus. Time for the meds no doubt. It was a shame as we wanted to swap rowing

Winners at Nottingham. From front left, Dave Sanfey, Richard Scott, Jarlath and John, and behind, Big Mac, Kieran, Rory, Dave Weale, and a surly author refusing to conform to the dress code (or absent mindedly not noticing what everyone else was wearing). The elegant footwear worn by all neatly encapsulates the era.

shirts. Wearing an East German rowing top on the Liffey would have ruled that sartorial roost.

Boy were they impressive physical specimens. All blond, tanned, muscular and at least 6 foot 5 inches, they seemed to have been taken straight out of Hollywood Central Casting's book of Leading Men. Shows you what a daily dose of cod liver oil can do for you.

And as for their rowing prowess generally, it was best summed up by Jarlath observing sourly to me, 'You know what your problem is Hickey? Six of the East German *women's* crew are bigger than you.'

Well, we had won an international race so what did I care about the world in the East.

2000 Metre Racing

The international rowing distance is two kilometres. Oddly, it is always described as 2000 metres in rowing land. Probably because it sounds a lot further, and when you're racing it certainly feels it.

Racing over that distance is truly horrible. It doesn't start too badly. You blast off the start at as high a rate of strokes per minute which the crew can manage cleanly and smoothly, and then hunt for the planned race rhythm and rate during the first 500 metres. It's all moving by so quickly, you don't really have time to think, and besides, the body is sucking in enough oxygen. So far, so good. You might sneak the occasional look to see how the opposition is doing but that is really the job of the cox and stroke in an VIII. For everyone else the priority is to search out that rhythm and get on with it. Eyes in the boat.

For the second 500 metres, you tend to hold the rhythm and just stay fixated on getting the technique perfect. In parallel, however, the body starts to mutter about the lack of oxygen.

The third 500 piece is awful. Dreadful. It tears your lungs out. It doesn't matter what level you are racing at. It is no man's land. It separates the mental and physical rowing wheat from the feeble chaff. It is too far out (except potentially for the very occasional winning Olympic crew) to dash for the end. The brain is screaming at you to hold something back for the last 500, but you know if you back off, the rivals will slide past. The lungs are starting to sear with pain, which escalates with every stroke, and yet you know you will have to lift it harder and higher in the last 500 metres. The mental pressure starts to climb exponentially. The weak brain is screaming at you:

'You can't hold this.'

'You've got to stop.'

'The bloody race doesn't matter.'

'Nothing matters except this awful pain and it's going to get worse, so stop now.'

There were times in races when I swore to God that if He got me out of the race there and then, I would never ever row again. That would be the deal.

In some ways, the third 500 is not you versus the other crews. It is you versus you. Somehow you have to drive the pain down the priority list and force the brain to stay focussed.

Catch the water cleanly at the start of the stroke as the oar drops in, keep the power on fully but smoothly through the stroke, and get that oar out smoothly and cleanly at the end of the stroke. Spin the oar around at the finish and try to get yourself and your seat to the top of the slide for the next stroke without disturbing the movement of the boat. Concentrate above the pain. Repeat, repeat, repeat without variation.

And then the last 500 arrives, but you can now count the strokes to the finish so you know it will end, and so the brain can dominate the emotion. It takes over again. You can push everything physically to the limit and beyond because brain logic is back in the ascendency and the pain and emotions are relegated as you work out whether what you have done will be enough to win it, and if you are down, whether there is anything you can do to nick it before the line.

Having said all of that, the third 500 is often where a race is won or lost. If you can hold the power and rhythm without sucking too much out of the crew's reserves, it can position you well for the final sprint to the line. If you let your race position slip, it is really hard to recover it in the final 500. On the other hand, if you blast through it, you need to be careful that you don't then fade away before the line.

The ideal of course is that you cross the line with nothing left. Not a single stroke able to be taken, but at the same time ensuring that every stroke taken up to the end holds the rhythm and the power. In reality, that can never be achieved. Everyone can always take one more. Or two more, or maybe three. Actually most people can take a lot more than the brain is telling them but it is never easy to believe that when the body is gasping for oxygen.

This is where racing experience comes in. The more one races, the more one gets used to thinking and performing under intense mental and physical pressure. But also, the more one races, the more one is sensitive to small relative movements in the competitors' boats.

With practice, a slight relative movement in the opposition's position will register, as also will a slight movement up or down in their rate. The skill in racing is to detect this the moment it happens.

If you detect you are slipping back, you have to do something to stop it, and ideally try to claw back the lost ground. If you detect you are moving ahead, then you have to quickly analyse what has caused it, and can it be reinforced.

It is no accident that most Olympic finals see the fastest crews overlapping at the finish. Instinctively, the experienced crews will know from practice the bare minimum that they have to do to stay close to the leader, or to stay just ahead of the field. The ultimate winner is the one who has best judged their own speed and endurance limit, against that of the other crews.

And the awful thing, the worst thing in the world, is getting to the finish line without winning and you ask yourself, could I have done more? If the answer to that question is no, then the result matters not. Win or lose, nothing more you could have done. It's life, it's racing, it's rowing. Sometimes you just come up against a faster crew.

But if the answer to that question should ever be yes, then you must leave the sport. It is not that anyone will necessarily know. The point is that you will know, and you know if you do it once, you will always do it, and you will never trust yourself.

And knowing that in advance means you can never, ever, give up, back off, ease off, take a breather. Never. People don't fall off rowing machines to try to convince others how hard they have tried. They fall off rowing machines because their body can no longer function to keep them on the seat. There is no alternative. You just can't stop. It is why people refer to it as a brutal sport. It is.

But if you are willing to pay that price, rowing will give you the mental and physical strength that will sustain you in all aspects of life.

That First House at Henley

So our first visit to the hallowed waters of Henley finally materialised. Someone had booked accommodation for us in a large house on the Oxford Road for the planned week. It was owned by a set of remote parents who we barely ever saw, but the place had a big garden and three lovely daughters.

One of the boys (because of what follows I had better call him Romeo) fell in love with the eldest immediately and set out to make an impact. Lots of his dreadful stories and 'jokes' quite ruined most mealtimes, but because he was obviously desperate to make an impression, we tolerated it.

The warm summer evenings after dinner were very pleasant as we all relaxed on the sofas around the television set, watching the international cricket match in a fine old drawing room whose doors opened out onto the lawn. It could have been idyllic really. And it was, for a while.

We were all in that fine old drawing room after supper one evening. Meanwhile, Romeo was out in the garden pushing wooden balls around the place with a wooden mallet, pretending he understood the rules of croquet, when he took a sudden urge and headed for us. Barrelling in, he swivelled around, placed both outstretched arms on the television, bent over and with careful aim, let off an outrageous fart in the direction of the largest sofa opposite.

Romeo was well built, and this emission lived up entirely to its creator's expectations. More Richter than Rectum in scale and size. It was a magnificent performance rivalling Jeremiah Clarke's 'Trumpet Voluntary', both in range and duration.

'Share that amongst you,' came the accompanying commentary.

Eventually (or so it seemed) the volcano subsided, and he turned around in triumph. It was only then he spotted her. The darling of the house, sitting demurely in the middle of the sofa with a fine silk scarf hastily brought up to cover her nose and mouth. It was a big scarf and it needed to be as her mouth was still wide open with shock. She was straight out of Jane Austin's *Persuasion* and was clearly struggling to adapt to *Strumpet* (or was it Trumpet?) *City*.'

We, in the meantime, were on the floor. Firstly, because there was some semblance of an oxygen supply at that low altitude, and secondly, because being so convulsed with laughter we were quite incapable of sitting upright.

Well there wasn't much he could do, and so he made the best of it. Sweeping into a low curtain call bow, he thanked us all profusely and, with magisterial bearing, gathered up his remaining self-esteem (which in fairness didn't take that long) and exited stage left back out into the garden. He was last seen blasting innocent croquet balls into the adjoining counties.

What a performance. What an exit. What a man. Shame really that he didn't get the girl. Surely a little Brut aftershave would have settled everything.

Racing for the First Time at Henry's Regatta

Henley Royal Regatta is a real anachronism. On the one hand it is a rowing mecca where many of the top crews from all over the world meet and compete for a multiplicity of trophies. And it is probably that which brings the competitors there; the chance to test oneself against the best. It caters for everyone from the fastest international crews to young school boys and girls.

The odd thing is that it is not a conventional six lane course, albeit it is straight. Two lanes only, and it is therefore more akin to Wimbledon in terms of having early rounds and then the various quarter and semi-finals leading on to the final race between the fastest two crews in each event. This means that the regatta is spread over most of the first week in July each year.

In parallel with the sporting side, entry to the social side is almost as sought after. ('You mean there is rowing going on as well?'). Different entry badges (as distinct from the less socially acceptable 'tickets') are required for each day, and there are various categories depending on whether or not one is a member, a guest or a competitor.

There is a strict dress code which has barely changed since the regatta was founded, but 'strict' has a different meaning to that which might be expected. Blazers are acceptable regardless of colour and condition. Accordingly, variations of every colour and combination under the rainbow are permitted. Frequently, for instance, universities will have a number of different colour codes depicting different levels of rowing seniority. This therefore makes it easy to identify one's former crew members and fellow former club members. Since new blazers imply a lack of rowing experience, and hence credibility, the older and more thrashed the coat, the more respected it is.

It also means of course that through the blazers and ties worn, one's rowing pedigree is on show for all to see, which is of course why the men in particular return year after year. Nothing like having an excuse to dress up as prize peacocks.

Strangers to the event can be taken aback, however. Years later we had some great German friends attending as our guests. He was an extrovert Bavarian by birth and nature, and she was a serious Prussian by breeding and intellect. We noticed that as the day went on, they became more and more quiet and reflective and we started to worry that something had gone seriously awry with their enjoyment of the day.

The answer came that evening. In Germany they explained that school friends assembling publicly in 'uniforms' and meeting year after year to celebrate their shared history was not really permitted, for obvious historical reasons. To see meetings overtly taking place between octogenarians wearing the same blazers came as a considerable shock to people brought up in an environment where common dress had unfortunate connotations. How little we sometimes know about our neighbours.

First Race, and Last Race

Meanwhile, here we were. The famous Henley Royal, and the Big Mac's target. We spent the first few days practicing, and then Thursday arrived and with it our first race on that hallowed water.

We did have one great advantage in the stern of the boat, apart from John. He sat in the stern facing him. Jarlath. Our cox. Driving a boat like this is not as easy as it may sound. Straight courses are hard enough to navigate. The rudders in modern rowing shells are tiny items, about the size of a couple of credit cards, and set well forward from the stern of the boat. They permit small adjustments at the best of times, and there is always a time lag before the adjustment made takes effect.

Moreover, Henley is different from most river race courses. While the rowing course set out on this reach of Father Thames is dead straight, the riverbank meanders in and out like a drunk heading to the bar for a refill. For a cox, it is very easy to watch the sides of the river instead of the floating booms which mark the course and which extend virtually its full length. Spectators at the regatta are always grateful to novice coxes for throwing in non-existent chicanes, just to keep the races more interesting. Jarlath thankfully had no such consideration for the crowds and always kept an impeccable straight line for us.

The water in the Henley Reach always feels different. It is not that the river flow is in any way particularly strong at that time of year. It feels rather as if it has slow, Pacific-like surges which appear to lift the boat from time to time. It may be that the specially placed wooden booms on either side of the course somehow corral the wakes arriving from the passing cruisers and the umpires' launches and compress them into a more manageable flow. Boats seem to bounce somewhat more than elsewhere. Either way, it always seemed to take us an outing or two to feel comfortable.

Yanked Out

Given the recent Nottingham evidence, we were not a bad crew, I thought, but even before we arrived at the boat tents, we were well aware that we were not a serious contender for the event that year. Which was just as well, really, because what we saw on the morning of our first arrival reduced us to utter silence.

The American crews were in town. They were loud, confident and carrying sleek brand new boats. At all times they seemed surrounded by coaches carrying their equipment for them, and pretty girls clearly admiring each and every one of them.

That was bad enough, but what was psychologically fatal to us were the crews themselves. To a man they were tall and wide, heavy and bronzed. Another selection from Hollywood Central Casting to make us feel inferior. Their kit was all bright colours, each crew with identical gear, and all marked up with their university or club name, and often the name or number of the individual oarsman. They positively oozed money, success and superiority.

And the accompanying girls. Oh my word. Each pretty as a peach and seemingly wanting no more from life than to gaze adoringly at their Adonises. Mind you, facing death from a wild boar (I had to look up what happened to young Adonis) didn't carry much appeal, so perhaps in some ways we were happy to leave them all to each other.

By contrast we were white, skinny and scared (well I was anyway). Our training kit was a mixture of colour, material and condition that any self-respecting landfill site would have rejected at the gate. Our once white woollen rowing shorts were a dull, damp, limp grey and hung shapelessly more or less around our rear ends. Actually less rather than more. Sagged is probably the word I'm looking for. What on earth are we doing here I thought. Let me back to the drizzle and cloud of Islandbridge. This will be embarrassing.

It got worse. The draw appeared and we had a seeded crew, the Massachusetts Institute of Technology, aka MIT, in the first race. Great. They won't have come all this way if they were a crew of sluggards. All that training only for us probably to meet the same fate as countless Trinity crews in countless previous Henleys.

The awful day loomed and there was nothing for it but to paddle up to the start and await our fate. I entirely understood Samuel Johnson's comment about hanging concentrating the mind wonderfully. We were told afterwards that we resembled startled rabbits as we waited for the umpire's starting litany, but I'm not sure we were that sturdy. I could barely breathe with fright and already knew this was going to hurt more than anything else in life. I did my usual deal with God.

'Get me through this and I swear I will never climb into a boat ever again,' but I think He must have been in the Fawley Bar with Noah, Captain Ahab, and maybe even Charon, waiting to transport the day's losers to their final aquatic destination.

I was always struck by the great Sir Steve Redgrave's comment *after* the famous Sydney win, when he invited anyone who saw him climb into another boat to shoot him. Had he said it before the race, I would have understood it.

I always forgot my religious deal when the race was finished no matter if we won or lost. If I and the crew had rowed well, I was always able to contemplate going again. Could it be that the aftermath of an Olympic Final was more stressful even than a Henley start? Perhaps, but I don't really think so.

A Start

Your first Henley start is designed to shrink every moveable organ and orifice in your body, and come to think of it, also the ones which you had always thought previously were immoveable.

The umpires come straight from the Noel Coward school of superior British beings, dealing with the lesser orders arriving from the Colonies who have deigned to appear in the mother country, and the Good Lord alone knows why.

In reality, of course, they are almost invariably the most decent of people, which is hardly surprising given that they are all former oarsmen (and these days oarswomen) who have competed successfully at a high level. (There, that ought to secure my membership of The Stewards' Enclosure for another year).

A Henley start, viewed from the umpire's launch

'*When I see that both crews are straight and ready, I shall start you like this. "Are you ready? Go." Get ready please.*'

It is not so much the words. It's the tone, and the lines are invariably delivered with, I must admit, the most marvellous accents reminding one of none other than David Niven, the right side of a bucket of Pimm's No.1 Cup.

What they mean by these hallowed words of course really is,

'*You miserable little worms have no breeding and are quite ruining my day, and the sooner I can get rid of you off up the course, and join my guests for tea, the happier I shall be. So get ready to be dismissed,*' or sentiments to that effect.

MIT were big and fast and fully justified their seeded status. The race started, and rather like they say about the

MIT beating the crew in Year One. This was taken shortly after the start of our first (and only) race in 1975 as we (on the left) led MIT. The narrowing course markers give some illustration of the distance to be travelled in each race.

1960s, in truth I can't recall a single detail. But I know I was there. The pain at the end confirmed it.

We lost. We led for the first two minutes, equalling the course record to the first marker, The Barrier, before being rowed through and losing by three quarters of a length. As we flashed (well, all right then, gasped) our way through the finish and then tried to recover in the boat, I was fed up that the club had again lost at Henley early in the regatta.

I was even more fed up to be beaten by a crew wearing identical and quite dreadful coloured baseball caps. Could we not at least be beaten by people with some sartorial taste?

It was only when Robin spoke to us after the race that we realised that actually we had been far faster than any previous Trinity crew, and in the context of the competition overall, our performance was far from shabby. As it turned out, MIT did not win the event but in knocking them out later in the week, the winners had to set a new record for the full course.

It still rankled though. All that year's hard training and commitment to be rewarded by a polite clap from the crowd as we lost. I concluded that I hated Henley and never wished to see the place again.

It was an utter outrage that a crew was allowed to row wearing matching baseball caps. The angle of the MIT oars however shows how hard we pushed them. They were all over the place at the end. Still ahead of us mind you, but at least we held our composure. It's more important to look right. Sure it is.

Year Two

Suits You, Sir

Again I returned to Trinity, and again I signed up for another repeat dose of training and pain. But had I known then what was in store, I'm not sure I would have made the same decision. If the first year had its wild moments, OMG this next year became seriously outrageous.

The term began with the Big Mac reminding us all that he was in his final year of law exams (which he would pass, become a very well-known and successful barrister and subsequently a judge). Accordingly, he used that pathetic excuse to drop out of active rowing. Mind you, I was secretly delighted with his enforced decision as he had occupied the 6 seat in Year One, which meant I could start daydreaming about being able to move up to 6 from the 4 seat, which I had occupied last season. Traditionally, the 5 and 6 seats are seen as the heart of the engine room of an VIII (though the reality at the top of the sport is that everyone in the boat is a veritable engine). I figured if I could end up there I would be difficult to dislodge.

The year's new captain was Dave Sanfey who moved quickly and smoothly to maintain the Big Mac momentum from October onwards. He made it quite clear that the Ladies would remain the target and he was personally determined to nail himself into the 3 seat in the VIII for that season. That was enough commitment for everyone else in the squad to return and have another crack at taking the Ladies.

I was a bit heavier that year and I was gaining confidence in life generally, and began the term looking forward to it all. It didn't last.

In Trinity, the Boat Club was generally reckoned to be the fittest of all the sporting clubs. So when the rugger buggers in their final year challenged their equivalents in my year, I was asked to play. Protests were to no avail, and so I showed duly showed up for the pre-match briefing the day before the game.

'Hickey, you're tall so we will throw the ball to you at the lineouts.'

I said, 'Okay, but do I have time to learn the codes you fellows use?'

'You're forgetting we are rugby players,' came the response.

'The winger (as it was in those days), throwing the ball in, will shout a series of numbers,' I was told.

'If his left foot is in front, it means the ball will be thrown to you. If his right foot is in front, it won't come to you. Do you know your left from your right?'

I bristled.

'Well, you're doing economics, aren't you? It's a reasonable question. Now feck off and find some kit. We're going drinking, I mean training.'

Yeah, sure you are.

I knew our treasurer, 'Financial Genius' Jim Jackson, used to play, so I asked to borrow his boots. FG Jim was, and remains, a serious financial player. Stories abound that he funded his entire university course through late night poker games, and it is not difficult to believe every word of that. Chosen by Big Mac to oversee the club's finances, he did so to a successful extent never seen before or since.

But back to the rugby kit. Regarding boots, Jim said, 'sure you can borrow mine, we're about the same size feet, and do you have a jockstrap?'

I thought, I'm not borrowing his, I know where it's been.

'Come on,' he said, 'let's go up Grafton Street to the sports store and buy you one.'

We searched all the shelves to no avail. Walking towards the sales counter, I suddenly cringed and backed away. The most gorgeous girl stood there confident and smiling at us.

'Can I help you boys?' This was far too embarrassing, and the 'boys' bit really stung.

'Men, if you please,' I said to myself, but only to myself. Jim was made of sterner stuff.

'Yeah, one jockstrap please.'

'Sure,' she replied still smiling, 'what size?'

Drawing himself up to his full height, swelling out his chest, and dropping his voice an octave, Jim said loudly *'Large.'*

I nodded supportively. She needed to know that we were real men. I could vouch for the pouch.

'Yes sir,' she said looking at him. She had dropped the smile. It had been replaced by a mile wide grin.

'We measure them by the waist, sir.'

Dear oh dear. That left both of us crimson. Time I stuck to rowing and time he got back to high finance.

Stoned in Derry

Robin was again in charge and early this season he decided we needed to keep sharp from a racing perspective. In parallel, he decided that we could do with an intensive training camp. He alighted on the Foyle Head for the former, so early in the season we headed north.

The Foyle Head takes place each year in Stroke City, otherwise known as Derry/Londonderry/Derry/Londonderry/Derry (repeat until politically correct) in early February and so off we went. For many of us, this would be a rare visit north of the border, and for some our first visit to that fine city. At the time it was very troubled and potentially dangerous, so the plan was to bus up from Dublin, row the race and then move on quickly that same day to our chosen training camp.

Disembarking the bus near the start, we assembled the boat, took to the water and almost immediately the race started. As we rounded a bend ten minutes or so later, in the middle of the race, we heard shouting and yelling.

'Fukin' Prods, go back where you belong,' and similar calls of endearment came at us from a bunch of fellows standing on a sand spit sticking out into the river. The shouts were followed by rocks heaved at us, splashing around the boat, but thankfully hitting neither craft nor crew. We sped away as fast as we could, which probably accounted for us managing to win the overall event.

In reality, of course, by then, Trinity was no longer a Protestant enclave and thus the great irony of the day was the fact that if the crew had to pick something religious to die on, it was more likely to be a Calvary Cross than a King James Bible. We were being stoned by 'our own sort'. It all felt a bit biblical, and so we didn't hang around much, and straight after the race quickly packed the boat onto the trailer.

We did think it a bit of a laugh, though, and decided that 'Join the Boat Club and Get Stoned' would have to feature in our future recruitments blurb. Our laughing didn't last that long. We had a temporary rowing coach with us, name of H (well not really H, but even today it would do him no favours to reveal his real name).

Very decently, he decided that we all deserved a pint after our win, and so at the edge of the city, he ordered the bus to be pulled over and we all spilled out into the selected bar. The pints were lined up and H was duly paying for them when we noticed the barman looking at H with a steady stare. After a moment he said very quietly, and somewhat menacingly, 'nice to see you back here Captain.' Those of us who heard it had no idea what was going on, but that quickly changed.

H said immediately, 'Boys, out now, let's go.'

We looked at him in complete confusion and not a little disappointment, but the firmness in his voice brooked no discussion. We piled straight on to the bus, which set off directly for Enniskillen. It was then that he explained that he had served in Northern Ireland with the British Army and was far from happy that he had been recognised. It was a real reminder to us innocents that the so called 'Troubles' were actually deadly serious. We were merely on the fringes.

Enniskillen Long Distance

Robin had selected this glorious location for an intensive week's training. Enniskillen was also Tom Noble's hometown, and we were delighted to see him take a keen interest in us throughout the week. By the end of the week that was something he was to regret.

The River Erne twists and turns its way through the western side of Northern Ireland for miles and miles, dallying for a time in two great big lakes, between which it flows firmly through the centre of the beautiful old town of Enniskillen. It is a truly perfect location if your ambition is to cover long rowing distances in a majestic setting. Basing ourselves in a row of little hotel chalets just outside the town, it didn't take us long to lower the tone of the entire county.

Robin knew what he wanted. We were to have two outings every day and then race the Erne Head of the River at the end of the week. Having selected his preferred crew for the season, he wanted to mould us into a unit. Part of the plan was therefore to send us out daily for lengthy periods of steady rowing. His thinking was that we would get so tired that we would be incapable of doing anything in the boat other than getting into a perfect rowing harmony. Some hope with this lot.

Without perfect synchronisation, rowing in crew boats just doesn't work, even if a crew has perfect individual technique and great fitness. All the crew have to put the power into the stroke at exactly the same moment, stroke after every stroke. This is not merely ensuring that entry and egress of the oars to and from the water has to involve perfect timing. Within the stroke itself while the oar is in the water, the power has to be applied evenly and equally throughout the boat. Long distances, practiced with an unchanged crew formation, are therefore deployed to eliminate minor differences of timing in the power application between crew members.

I suspect that is why East Coast American crews usually look so drilled when the summer racing season arrives. They spend the frozen winters practicing indoors in rowing tanks, being intensively coached to replicate each other's strokes until they are indistinguishable.

Personally, I can't think of anything more boring than spending the winter sitting in a shed being yelled at by a coach pretending to be the usual demented Marine Corps drill instructor bawling at his raw recruits.

Back in Enniskillen, being early in the year, the Irish weather was of course all over the place, well capable of delivering an amuse bouche of each season during a single outing. Rain wasn't an issue as it tended to keep the water flat. Cold was manageable as we layered up and had (finally) learnt what worked warmth-wise, and what didn't. Snow was pretty and sunshine was welcome.

Wind is always the big enemy of rowing. Rowing shells are low to the water and, as we now know, even foot high waves can readily swamp a crew. We did have to sit out the occasional session as the wind blew down the river making it impossible to risk an outing. Still better than sitting in a shed being bawled at though.

There was one especially glorious day when Robin sent us off to row several hours on our own as he caught up with old friends who lived locally. Instructed to bring food and water, we set off in the morning from our base on the edge of the river, a few miles south of Enniskillen town. Passing under the centre bridge of the town, we rowed on north into the Lower Lough Erne and continued north for nigh on twelve miles or so. Up there the scenery is stunning and, as luck would have it that day, there wasn't a cloud in the sky.

We paddled on and on and on, passing a myriad of little green and empty islands as we seemed to move further and further away from all signs of life and civilisation. Eventually, seeing one of these deserted Robinson Crusoe-type islands with a gentle beach, Jarlath steered us in. We hopped out, lifted the boat from the water and sat down happily do what oarsmen do best, which is to talk utter rubbish and eat everything in sight. It was one of those days when we all understood why we bothered with this daft sport.

Overall, though, it was a tough and tiring week, but we were clearly improving as a crew. Our stamina and technique came on very considerably, and we could all sense that the boat was moving better and better as the week went on. It was therefore no great surprise when race day came around and we turned out to be the fastest crew over the course.

The Bloody Barrel

We were actually pretty elated having won and headed straight back to base for din dins. The chalets where we were billeted were part of a local hotel. It was quite a sought after venue, positioned beautifully as it was on the shores of the river. After nosebags, we deployed to the hotel bar, which was at one end of the posh dining room. It was the fourteenth of February.

We had been given an immediate training break and so everyone hit the beer. Of course, if you don't ordinarily take alcohol, it doesn't take much to send you flying.

Several Trinity crews of varying seniority had joined us for the week, and a few individuals stamped their mark. John was an early hero. The hotel dining room, positioned right by the bar, was decorated in a mad 1960s style of Hollywood Hawaii, with plastic swaying palm trees, umbrella cocktails on the menu, and red and yellow colours everywhere. I think the style could best be termed 'gruesome'.

John knocked back a few pints and then fancied a walk up a palm tree, as you do. He actually did rather well for a time until the bending palm got tired of him, and suddenly went over all horizontal. Gravity deposited him onto the nearby couple's table. The male half of the couple didn't react so well to having his big Valentine's Day seduction dinner deposited on his lap, presumably preferring that his lady for the evening would fulfil that role in due course. Quite unreasonably, it seemed to us, he started whingeing to the management and, totally unfairly, and quite inexplicably it seemed to us innocents, we were all requested to exit the hotel bar immediately.

Somewhat cross about this and still thirsty, a deputation slunk around the back of the building and quickly liberated a large aluminium keg of Harp lager. With much glee and no co-ordination, this prize was unsteadily rolled down the hill to the first of the riverside chalets.

There then followed a most frustrating period while every attempt to access the pressurised 88 pints of liquid gold within was heroically resisted by this tough receptacle. In desperation, Anis Sadek (a devilishly handsome mix of Mayo and Middle Eastern breeding which had also produced in him strong lateral thinking capability) left the chalet and returned with what can only be described as a very large cross, seemingly constructed of pig iron.

The engineers in the party consulted when they saw this apparition appear and cautiously recommended that the chosen weapon ought best be deployed in the bath, to prevent the precious liquid being lost in case matters did not go entirely to plan. The economics undergraduates amongst the crews said it couldn't be done and foretold a recession.

Nonetheless, a dozen thirsty 'helpers' squashed into the smallest room in the chalet, and one of the medics did actually remember to put the plug in the bath. Clearly, their training included the closing of all orifices before serious operations. The chosen barrel was then carefully placed upright in the bath and, like a demented Moses, Anis rose up, stood on the side of the bath, and launched the iron missile at the barrel valve. All things considered, it was an excellent strike.

There were several outcomes. The most minor of these was that on the upswing, the rising cross penetrated the ceiling of the bathroom, struck a rafter, and a quantity of wood, plaster and dust descended over everyone. The cross then reversed direction and headed south at maximum velocity. It hit the valve, middle stump.

Possibly next in the scale of outcomes was that the principal component (namely, the bath itself) of the totally cool, top of the range, avocado-shaded bathroom suite failed utterly to cope with Anis' strike. With a loud crack, the bath shattered, depositing Anis in a heap on the floor, and as he went, he dragged virtually everyone down with him. As it turned out, this was no bad interim result.

I say this because by far the most noticeable outcome was that the stunning iron strike had the effect of forcing the valve straight down into the beer barrel. This instantly depressurised the barrel, which celebrated wildly by taking off in exultation and careering around the room at an insane speed.

It hit and smashed one wall but was only getting started. Blasting a huge volume of orange lager from its tail like some biblical comet, it crashed around the room bouncing off the walls, the ceiling, the now vacated floor (the engineers having been first out of the room, followed by the economics undergraduates declaring that they had been correct all along). It clearly disliked avocado as it rapidly demolished the toilet bowl and then the sink. By way of a penultimate celebration, though by now with weakening effort, it attacked the window and shattered the glass. Finally, however, with its power waning, it tried but failed to escape the room, which by now was inches deep in the amber nectar.

Outside the bathroom, there was an understandable and somewhat lengthy silence before Dave Weale was heard to mutter, 'Harp is a shite pint anyways, so nothing lost there.'

An immediate committee meeting was held, and the unanimous recommendation from the engineers was that it would be best if the evidence of this little adventure were to be covered up. The economists worried more about the hotel's annual trading margins, but didn't otherwise contribute. And so without further ado, the now empty keg was retrieved from its resting place, brought out into the fresh air to sober up, and then carefully tossed as far out into the river as two drunken engineers could manage on a slippery grass slope in complete darkness. Which is to say it flopped into the water some six inches off the bank. It was enough. The last we saw of it, it was floating contentedly away in the general direction of Enniskillen town.

Next morning we set off back to Dublin, leaving Tom and the coaches to explain to the hotel manager what they couldn't explain – the calamity that had befallen the chalet bathroom – but offering to return again next year as compensation.

Later that week a letter arrived at Boat Club rooms. It was A4 sized and carried a stamp with the Queen's head on it. Intrigued, we opened it and saw within a terse note from Tom, together with a newspaper. The note said, 'see the front page'. The paper was *The Impartial Reporter*, a weekly printed in Enniskillen. The lead article described how a few days previously, the British Army had detected a large metal object wedged against the bridge in the middle of Enniskillen town and, deeming it to be very suspicious, had removed and detonated it safely in a remote location. It is reportedly still a mystery. Not to us it isn't. Gulp.

Breakfast on the Hoof

Since John was taking time out for his final engineering exams, I again slipped into the stroke seat of the boat. The annual Dublin Head of the River arrived and we managed to win it. Being the last head race of the year, the date heralded a week's training break. There was a party at the Boat House in honour of something or other, so several of us returned there in the evening to celebrate. We all had exams looming, however, so we were rather restrained alcohol-wise. We did make a long night of it nonetheless, relaxing and chattering away.

Daylight appeared and we all realised we were seriously hungry. Two of the lads suggested breakfast at the local hotel. I demurred citing lack of money, but then someone said he'd stand me. A third chap had the father's big Cortina so we piled in and found our way there just as they were opening up for breakfast. The hotel is long since gone, but it had been quite swish.

We headed up into the empty restaurant and took the stools at the bar, looking directly into the kitchen. The chef gave us a cheery welcome and the head waiter appeared behind the counter and distributed the menus.

'Won't need these,' said one lad. 'Full Irish all round,' and we all nodded approvingly. We knew well the relativities surrounding 'full' breakfasts and wouldn't have settled for anything less than an 'Irish'. It has nothing to do with location or nationalities, and all to do with ingredients.

Breakfast is important stuff to rowers, and a 'full' one is essential. However there are variations on the theme. Lowest, I'm afraid, is a Full English. This is thin fare at the best of times. It comprises merely bacon, egg, sausage, tomato and mushrooms. Occasionally baked beans will be added to make it appear fuller, and possibly even some fried bread, though in these healthy days this is relatively rare. Honestly, it is never worth the money.

The Ulster Fry is a significant step up the gourmet ladder, adding black pudding, potato bread and soda bread to everything English, and improving it accordingly.

Top of the stack comes the Irish. To the Ulster Fry must be added white pudding, these days, hash browns and, in proper establishments, possibly a decent slice of liver. If an Ulster Fry is usually described as a heart attack on a plate, the Full Irish is a veritable pandemic.

On this occasion, there was no doubt in my mind that we would each do justice to the chef's expected fine work. My only uncertainty was whether one of the lads might just order two.

The feasts duly appeared and were despatched in record time, alongside a loaf of the finest preserved full white bread, and pots of butter, marmalade and tea. Each, near as dammit.

The bill appeared and I quickly passed it around. It was carefully studied and then the old 'slap the empty pocket routine' started up. I felt distinctly weak. My pocket really was empty. The joke wore off quite quickly and all four of us looked at each other. OMG, there was no one able to pay.

There followed much faked sighing and someone said, 'Plan B then.'

'Plan B it is,' the others all nodded.

As far as I was concerned they were speaking Walloon, but I was thinking more of balloons going up shortly and a mound of last night's hotel dinner dishes looming.

'What's Plan B?' I asked.

'Hickey, sit there until I tell you to move and then do exactly what I do,' said one helpfully, and the others nodded.

One lad rose languidly, exchanged a few pleasantries with the head waiter, and ambled off to the jacks. (This is Irish for lavatory. It is named after Jack Power, the man who discovered shit in Ireland, and a seat through which to deposit it. I know he did both because despite considerable research and related detective work, I can find no other mention of shit in Irish history, so it must have been him. I did a lot of work on this topic. 'No shit Sherlock' you might call me.)

After a short interval, another lad headed the same way, and in parallel, out of the corner of my eye, I saw the first lad (our driver) amble out of the jacks and head towards the most elegantly glazed front revolving door of the hotel. I felt the tension building in me as I started to realise what Plan B really meant. The last of the three was chatting amiably to the chef across the bar, looking as if butter wouldn't melt in his mouth. Mind you, having eaten most of the hotel's weekly supply, there wasn't much butter left around to melt in any event.

The second lad emerged and moved quietly but swiftly towards the front door as the chef turned away to check his vol au vents, or whatever it is that chefs check. Maybe his trousers were a bit too tight.

It then all happened so fast. I got a slap on the arm and was told 'showtime'. The last lad (apart from me) took off for the revolving front door at some speed. I was a bit slower until I heard a yell from the head waiter, immediately followed by a louder yell from the chef, following which I upped the rate markedly and arrived at the revolving door at the same time. Thinking I was obeying his command to do as he did, I went into the opposite side of the revolving door. We both slammed up against the glass on either side which, somewhat unsportingly, refused to budge.

Meanwhile, outside through the elegantly glazed glass, I could see that the car had been reversed towards the door with three doors open, and the second lad was already halfway into the front seat.

The last man, weighing at least a stone more than me and being a darn sight stronger, prevailed in the revolving trial of strength and pushed his way out. I was spun around and dumped unceremoniously on the ground outside. I scrambled up, dived for the rear seat of the now moving car and was hoiked in unceremoniously.

'Chrissakes, Hickey, keep up,' came the growl as the driver hit the exit, swung the wheel and headed away.

As I recall, we went directly to one of the lads' parents' place where his admiring mother met us with her usual warm welcome and insisted that we should sit down and have breakfast as we were bound to be hungry, what with having had such an early start and all that morning.

The Infamous San Raf Party

Now by this time FG Jim had left college and secured a senior position in an investment bank in Dublin. In this role he was meeting dozens of corporates eager to expand their Irish operations. One such had come up with a potential plan to distribute an alternative to that alcoholic red soup known to the world as Dubonnet. Jim cleverly sold the chosen Irish distributor of this new bevy the concept of sponsoring the Trinity Regatta and thus accessing the finest of Irish society. A bit farfetched, but they went for it, big time.

On the day, a monster juggernaut rolled up, and crates and crates full of bottles containing the newly created St Raphael wonder drink arrived at the regatta enclosure tents and were passed out to all and sundry for free. Because of this astute pricing strategy, vast quantities were consumed, albeit somewhat sheepishly it must be said. Real men drank Guinness, and oarsmen are 'real men', well at least in their own minds. But if you offer them a sixteen per cent alcohol freebie when their racing is done for the day, you will need to stand well back when inevitably they decide 'it would be a rude thing not to taste a few crates of the stuff'.

Despite this largesse and related indulgence, by the end of the regatta there still remained an EEC-sized lake left over. What to do with it? Jim was nervous of admitting to the distributors that there was a surplus as it might suggest that it hadn't been that popular. As he was pondering this conundrum, I happened to wander past.

'Hickey,' he said. 'You have rooms in Front Square do you not?'

'Yes,' I replied truthfully.

'Well you're having a party. Don't argue. It will be the night of Trinity Ball.'

I paid no attention, vaguely wondering what he was blathering on about.

The Boathouse adorned with a San Raf banner prior to their sponsorship of that year's Trinity Regatta. The tall man with the bushy hair is none other than Anis Sadek, he of the infamous Enniskillen beer keg escapade.

Party Central (note the serious faces): David Sanfey as Captain, Jim Jackson, our financial genius, Alva Brangam, the master of taste, and a representative from San Raphael distributors.

The afternoon of Trinity Ball arrived. Not then having a steady girlfriend (actually I didn't even have an unsteady girlfriend, which I think would have been far more interesting), I didn't bother paying for a ticket, knowing that as I lived in Front Square, I would be able to attend without paying and, you never know, I might meet someone.

Now Trinity Ball was the social and (potential) sexual highlight of the year. Every student wanted to go, and every male student reckoned this was the night he would get lucky and get laid. It was a black tie event, the college was sealed off from Dublin's external riff raff, and most of the exquisite classical buildings had their breeding temporarily tarnished by the arrival of Ireland's current rock and pop groups. To be fair to them, the organising committee usually delivered big time, and even Thin Lizzie and Geldof's effing Boomtown Rats were featured (I think) that year.

I got back to my rooms that Saturday afternoon after the usual double training outings. At about 3.00 pm there came a loud banging on the door, and my ever patient roommate Big Kieran Corrigan opened the outer door (we had two bedrooms and a lounge in our set up). He stood back aghast as FG Jim and five bulky oarsmen clattered past him ('Howya Big K') carrying, in no particular order, crate after crate after crate of San Raf, a few crates of lemonade, multiple plastic sacks of ice, dozens and dozens of pint glasses, and bags and bags of what appeared suspiciously like mint and marshmallows. Mint and marshmallows? WTF?

'What the fuck?' said the previously patient Big K.

'Hickey,' he bellowed. I came out of my room and stood there nonplussed.

'What the fuck?' he repeated. I had no idea what the fuck.

I looked at Jim and said, 'what the fuck?'

You could tell that we were the cream of Ireland's intellectual society, well used to forensic thought and eloquent discussion, having obviously benefitted enormously from the finest educational establishment in the land.

Jim immediately passed the buck to Alva Brangam. Apart from being one of the most able law students ever to grace Trinity, Alva in his spare time was the organisational genius who had transformed the annual Trinity

Regatta into a Henley look alike. I immediately twigged that he would have been in on this mad caper from the beginning. I know I'm right because only Alva would have had the class to think of mint and marshmallows.

'Your party, sir,' said Alva, and I suddenly remembered what I had dismissed as Jim's irrelevant blathering at the regatta.

'Oh shit,' was my considered response, looking at my roommate.

'I can explain.'

'I have no doubt,' said Big K looking at me somewhat witheringly and, stomping off into his bedroom, he rocked the door on its hinges. He could see what was brewing, or not brewing, if you will. Ouch.

Now Big K was not a rowing man. He could have been, but he preferred football, at which he excelled. More than that, he excelled academically and had the nerve to undertake two primary degrees, Business Studies and the legal qualification of an LLB, simultaneously. Somewhat depressingly for those of us who struggled with one degree, he achieved high grades in both. But it did mean he required serious study time and frivolous parties during term were not likely to assist in this.

I retreated back into my room and, unbeknownst to me, the professionals set to work in the lounge. I woke in the cot after my post-outing sleep to hear a babble of conversation and the unmistakeable clink of glassware. I wandered out into the lounge.

Holy shit, the place was set up as a full time bar with a bunch of lads serving pints to more and more arriving rowing and non-rowing types. It wasn't just men, there was a serious showing of girls, all beautifully turned out for the ball, and the lads all in black tie. I looked carefully at the pints. They had filled the glasses two-thirds with lemonade, one-third with San Raf, and then banged in the ice, mint and marshmallows on top.

'Aaten and drinkin' in it,' said one loutish novice oarsman who I pretended not to recognise.

'Tanx for a grand party,' he said, grinning inanely. I concluded he was not on his first crate.

More and more students arrived until my rooms looked exactly like, well, exactly like a student's rooms offering free alcohol for the night. The Black Hole of Calcutta would have seemed sparsely populated by comparison, had any of us known what that was. Come to think of it, that's exactly what it was, apart from the location obviously. The place was filling and filling. As we all know, word of free booze passes amongst a student body faster than promises pour from a politician.

I said to myself, this is nuts. Big K had sensibly barricaded his room, and though I suspected he had installed his then girlfriend as a better looking alternative to a scholarly analysis of the famous legal case known as 'Suisse Atlantique', I thought his pre-planning somewhat intelligent.

And They Say Romance is Dead

As for me, I thought I had better get out. As it happened, I had met up with a classmate earlier that week and (somewhat astonishingly for me) had asked her whether or not she was going to the ball. To my surprise, she said that she had intended to go, and had a ticket, but that her then boyfriend had wandered off to someone else. She asked whether I was going, and I said that since I was living within the confines, I had little choice but to attend and would happily meet her inside.

Just as I was planning to leave the party for some air, she arrived. I fought my way back into my rooms, leading the way to the San Raf source. She downed a pint of the lethal concoction, munched on the ice cubes and marshmallow, threw me out of my bedroom while she changed into a seriously mature (read very revealing) evening dress, and emerged wanting to party. Happy days.

We went out into Front Square and I don't remember a thing after that until in the small hours of the morning I recall we were sitting together on the communal stairs outside my rooms.

There was a reason we were sitting on the communal stairs. We could not get into my rooms for the simple reason that I was so smitten when she arrived that I clean forgot to take my key as we left the rooms. Idiot. Pounding on the door resulted in a bruised fist and little else, and so we sat there, actually quite happily chatting away as you do at that age. Boy can students talk some volumes of rubbish. I fear we were up there with the best of them.

At length, the outer door to my rooms opened, and a figure staggered out. Peering at me, or more accurately squinting somewhat in my broad general direction, and grinning contentedly, FG Jim (for it was he) said 'Saall yours' and fell off down the stairs. I thought, at last, the big seduction scene. Happy nights.

It was not to be. We went in and I opened the door to my bedroom and couldn't believe my eyes. Reilly looked up, lying on his back, in my bed, on my pillow, and had the nerve to say, 'Hiya Dave.'

Sprawled across him wearing skimpy knickers and little else, but fast asleep, was a very good looking girl. I couldn't bloody believe it. In my bloody bed. The dirty hound. How could he? He wasn't even embarrassed. He gave me a thumbs up. I gave him two fingers.

In desperation, I went into the lounge and what I found there can only be described as carnage. I discovered later that the supplies of ice, mint, marshmallows, lemonade and pint glasses had all run out well before the lake of San Raf had dried up. So people were 'forced' to neck the stuff directly from the bottle. And boy did they do so.

The floor was strewn with bodies heaped on top of one another. Male, female, it was almost impossible to tell which was which; they were three deep high. All totally out of it. Honestly, it looked like someone had come in with a bunch of Uzi machine guns and sprayed the entire room. And over this serious wreckage I swear there was a red fog of San Raf fumes. My friend looked in.

'What in God's name has gone on here?' she said.

'Not sure they ran out of the San Raf in time,' I said.

'We can't stay here,' she said and led me away to her place to talk more rubbish. At least that's all I'm saying. It was only 4.00 am or so …

Later that Morning

Back in the real world of rowing life, Robin was not sure about the makeup of the four bow men in the VIII. Accordingly, he had decided on some seat racing for that Sunday morning and so we were all on parade at Islandbridge at eight am.

All rowers will know that if done correctly, seat racing can determine who blends best with whom in a boat. It is not always solely about fitness, strength and technique, though they are each required. If a rower has all of those but is microscopically out of synch with the rest of the crew, the boat can be slower than should otherwise be the case.

So Robin had chosen a benchmark four, which I was to stroke, and with me were Reilly (I was no longer calling him Rory after last night), Dave Weale and Richard Scott. Richard was a superb athlete and sat in the boat for both the 1975 and 1976 seasons. Finishing his degree in 1976, he departed for the real world, however, thus allowing Ted to step into his place for the final season. John was to stroke the other boat, and behind him one man of the other three would be swapped in and out every other race.

We did four races, each being the full downstream course of about a mile. While we won every race, after the first my lungs were seared and I was seriously concerned that I could not last another one, never mind three more. It turned out that we four all felt equally knackered, and so we took the decision to try to get some greater run into the boat between strokes through rating slightly lower. In other words, we were going to try to let the boat do more of the work.

Of course, part of the reason we were so tired after the first race was that we were so pumped up with testosterone and adrenaline that we had been pulling at 110 per cent effort and had virtually blown ourselves up.

So we told ourselves that we would dial back the adrenaline. In fact, the adrenalin had vaporised after the first race. It was then that we realised that we had all been to the ball, but we didn't get into further detail. I still wasn't speaking to Reilly. A theory was developing amongst us, however, that perhaps we had enjoyed too much bed and not enough sleep. It turned out that the others, the bow quintet, had all been early to bed, as should have been the case for everyone, before seat racing. We, the stern IV, were well out of order.

I don't know how we survived the remaining three races, but we got through them and at the end Robin pronounced himself satisfied that his rotation exercise had settled in his mind which was the best bow four. We were all in the Long Room as he said this, and it was only then that he looked at my crew more closely. We were obviously shattered and could barely stand.

'You fellows don't look so good,' he said, and we shifted uncomfortably. Now Robin was nothing if not perceptive and he studied us carefully, and then raised a quizzical eyebrow.

The silence became very uncomfortable. Richard, being the bravest soul of us all, said,

'Sorry Robin, but I went to the ball last night.'

I could imagine instantly that 'oh shit' was written across the faces of the rest of us. Robin looked carefully at each of us.

'Anyone else get there as well?' he enquired steadily.

Shamefacedly, we all nodded. I thought to myself, this is going to get ugly. Robin was nothing if not scrupulously committed, and he demanded no less of everyone he encountered. But, as ever, he surprised us.

'Each of you fellows went to the ball?' he asked.

Silence.

'Did you get any sleep at all? Well that's a stupid question I guess,' he said, no doubt recalling his own undergraduate days.

There was a long silence and then, to our astonishment he suddenly smiled and said,

'Right, that's it for today, you've all done enough, get home and get some sleep.'

There were three lessons that came out of that exercise. Firstly, I started to realise that one could do a lot more physically if mental blockages were removed. If you had told me beforehand that I would be able to undertake four seat races without much sleep, I would not have believed you.

Secondly, Robin immediately recognised that by then we all had a level of fitness and strength that entirely vindicated his and Chris' training programme.

And thirdly, and somewhat dangerously for the VIII as a unit, the selected bow four concluded that their stern 'colleagues' were an arrogant bunch that thought themselves better than them. It wasn't actually true. We were not arrogant. Just better. Actually, to be honest, I'm not sure we were any better. Ours was a settled crew whereas the fellows in the other boat had to adapt to each other at very short notice as they swapped men in and out, and they would all undoubtedly have been on edge throughout.

Sanfey voiced the thought everyone had, 'Jesus Christ,' he said, 'and you feckers still beat us in every race?'

We thought it was a funny comment until we saw the looks on their faces. Time to shut up, behave, and think of the full crew.

How to Get Barred from a Dublin Bar

It was a Saturday evening and I decided to have my allotted pint somewhere different. I was still being allowed one Guinness every night in a desperate attempt to keep my weight up. Immediately outside the Front Gate I saw Piddles Maxwell lounging on the railings chatting to Luke Griffin, the rugby coach and former rower.

'Howya Dave, fancy a pint? My date hasn't appeared.'

Why did everyone call me 'Dave'? What was wrong with my full given name? I suppose it could have been worse. I have a friend who had a generally disliked colleague name of Rick. 'Silent P' they used to say when introducing him …

'Sure, I said.' We weren't close, he being some years ahead of me and not a rower. Luke said he would join us later. We went into the first bar in Suffolk Street (but you will have to guess from which end – I wouldn't mind going back there some day).

Now Piddles had something of a short fuse and a reputation for dodgy behaviour when a bit boozed. There
was a clue in that nickname. So I reckoned I would keep
it to one drink. Too late. He wolfed his down and headed
back to the bar to order a second. It was then I realised
that he must have been well oiled even before we had
met.

Maxwell had quite a posh accent and one of the lads at
the bar (Mouth One) tried to show off by mimicking him
to his friends as he was ordering the second round. I noticed with relief that Maxwell seemed to join in the banter
but was nonetheless standing oddly, facing the side of his
tormentor with one hand seemingly in his own pocket.

Relief was the right word. As Piddles left the bar and
headed back towards me, there was an almighty roar as
Mouth One suddenly felt a wet leg and simultaneously
realised what Maxwell had done. Peeing into someone
else's pocket was his speciality. Mouth One launched
himself at Maxwell in an uncontrolled fury.

Maxwell was light of frame and quick of foot, and he
neatly ducked out of the way. This resulted in Mouth
One crashing into me as I sat innocently at the table, and
the pair of us ended up on the floor. It was obvious to me
by then that I was in just as much trouble as Piddles since
Mouth One clearly thought he might as well hammer
me as my friend and drew his fist back. In desperation I
threw an arm up for protection and somehow my elbow
hit a nose in just the right, or wrong, spot, depending on
whose nose it was.

It was his. The eyes watered and his nose started to
gush snot and then blood and all the while I was slipping

away out of his grasp as fast as a cowardly eel coated in olive oil. By then our table was broken, several glasses lay smashed on the floor, the barman was yelling blue murder, the Mouth's First Mate and the rest were lining up for round two and I was slowly starting to think what on earth have I got myself into now?

I slithered away and was scrambling desperately for the door, with Piddles a few strides ahead, when I felt my collar grabbed from behind. Oh-oh. I put my head down, got pushed to one side and suddenly I was free. Griffin had arrived at the door, taken in the situation instantly, and landed a rugby player's handshake straight into the face of the First Mate. That caused the remainder of his gang to pause, during which time all three of us crashed out through the door and out into the street.

'Youze are barred,' was the oath yelled at us by the barman as the door swung closed behind us. Shame I thought, that looked like good entertainment, provided Griffin was on my side at all times.

Sheep

In reality, my first serious encounter with booze came a little later that year. We had competed against our rival university, UCD, in the annual race under the Liffey bridges, down through the centre of the city. Held at high tide, it is a spectacular and long course, with narrow arches making accurate coxing vital.

For the first time in aeons (or so I told everyone afterwards), we won it, and as stroke of the boat I was elated. After the usual celebratory dinner, pints started flowing and I sank more and more. Eventually, I couldn't look at further volume. Some 'kind' soul recommended whiskey but after the first mouthful I said no more please.

'So what do you like?'

I said, 'Fanta Orange,' so that's what they gave me, but only after the sneaky bastards had tucked the whiskey inside and told me it would be fine.

I have no recollection of matters thereafter until I woke the following day in my rooms. I have no idea how I got there. It was Sunday, and to my astonishment it was already three in the afternoon. That wasn't the only shock, however. Firstly, my head felt dreadful. It was as if someone was trying to grind off the top two inches with a blunt saw. Secondly, my mouth and throat felt like a dried out jockstrap. But that was only the start. College was quiet. I parted the curtain and peered out on to Front Square, which my rooms for Year Two overlooked.

Sheep. Everywhere was sheep. The Front Square was covered in sheep. All over the place. On the grass. On the cobbles. In the doorways. Shocked, I dropped the curtain, downed a pint of water, and went straight back to the cot. Slowly, I worked out what my 'friends' had done to the Fanta.

I woke again at 6.00 pm. No blunt saw and the jockstrap throat felt reassuringly damp, but I was still traumatised by the sight of the sheep. Gingerly, I opened the curtain and took a quick look. No sheep. Nothing. Nobody. I resolved never again to go within a thousand yards of a whiskey bottle and determined never to mention it to anyone. I never had a repeat, and over the years gradually the acuteness and worry of it all faded.

Front Square at Trinity College, minus the sheep

Years later I was flying back from a business trip to Chicago, and to pass the time I idly flicked on to a Sean Connery film called *The First Great Train Robbery*. With Donald Sutherland and Lesley-Anne Down, it looked a good bet to while away the hours. And indeed it was. Especially when the wily Ms. Down contrived to rescue her husband, Sean, just as he left the courthouse having been severely sentenced for train robbery. To effect his escape, she flooded the streets outside the courthouse with sheep and, having a fast carriage, dragged him aboard. They clattered along the cobblestones, across Front Square, and out the Front Gate of Trinity College. After all those years. What a relief. I asked the stewardess for a whiskey to celebrate.

Back to Henley for the Second Time

Robin concluded that our early exit the previous year had stopped us from getting familiar and comfortable with the Henley set-up. Accordingly, he decided that in parallel with entering the VIIIs again for the Ladies event, he would also enter a coxless IV in the Visitors Cup, also reserved in those days for university crews. The coxless would comprise the same configuration as that selected for the seat racing, namely, three from the stern of the VIII being me, Weale, Rory and the bowman, Richard. I was to stroke it and Rory was to steer.

Of all the possibilities in crew boats, coxless IVs and quad sculls are perhaps the two most enjoyable to row, provided the crews blend. Following the sleepless seat racing a few weeks earlier, our coxless IV was not so much blended as welded together. The thing seemed to fly along when asked.

We took to the Henley water after the training outings for the VIII and quickly adapted to the bouncy conditions. Our big worry was the early part of the race. While the course is buoyed immediately after the start, the buoys soon give way to long and stout wooden booms floating between equally stout upright stakes. The stakes are beaten into the riverbed and stand well over six feet above the water level. The booms move up and down a little with the water level while tethered by metal hoops to the stakes. The stakes are about as moveable as the heads on Easter Island.

You might get away with scraping an oar (in extremis, a boat) against the booms if you drift off the racing line.

But bang an oar seriously against a stake and your ribs will crack first as the boat slews around prior to stopping dead in the water. Not recommended.

So Rory was quick to step up and volunteer for the feared steering responsibility. Mind you, that was only after the other three of us had chorused 'no effing way am I doing it'. Steering in coxless boats is done via one built-in shoe of the selected rower's pair being free to angle left or right. Two thin steel cables run from the top of the shoe to the rudder, thus controlling its direction. It does require concentration not to move it the wrong way at the wrong time.

Rory clearly wasn't certain of the relative sturdiness of our oars though, and so during our first outing he managed to test them by whacking both oars on bow side against different stakes, and one on stroke side, rendering them all but useless. Our boatman, the skilled cabinet maker Albert Eakins, doing a pretty convincing impression of Mutley, the permanently muttering cartoon character, nevertheless went to work overnight repairing them, and did his usual careful craftsman's job. Rory was asked politely the following day whether he wouldn't mind according them some respect. He was only half listening and so proceeded to whack only one on our next run.

Where Fish Do It

Water is funny stuff. Rowers tend to need a lot of it, and not just for drinking. They prefer to sit on calm versions of it if they are to develop their technique.

I always found it surprising, whether rowing or in later years coaching, how far technique could advance if the oarsmen were able solely to focus on it, and not need to watch out for the surrounding terrain.

The best water is canal water (including even the Suez). Not tidal, so no rise or fall to watch out for. Rarely so wide as to attract much lateral wind, and more often than not (at least outside Holland), less populated by other craft and so less trailing wash to disturb a racing shell. And as for steering a coxless craft, it is child's play compared to the twisting vagaries of river courses. Lakes and specially built water centres/rowing courses can also be conducive to technique focus.

Rivers are tougher, and perhaps none more so than that stretch of the Thames below Richmond Lock in London known as the Tideway. Richmond is the last lock before the river flows into the menacing North Sea. Twice a day the river will fall and rise, sometimes by as much as 24 feet. For those of us non-engineers who cannot measure anything, that's about as much as three and a half rowers laid in a row. (It was Dorothy Parker who said once that if all the hookers in the world were laid end to end, she wouldn't be a bit surprised. Finally. I've been trying to get that line in since I started this book.)

The Thames flow reverses accordingly with the changing tide and strict rules are in place for rowing boats to cope with the changing conditions. Rowers can work the so-called 'slacks', being the areas by the edge of both river banks. This is necessary since in winter, especially after heavy rainfall, a falling tide can readily make it impossible for even a fast VIII to make it upriver in the centre of the stream. Hugging the shoreline will keep the craft out of the main flow and allow progress against the elements.

However the slacks reverse in line with the changing tide. But the tide doesn't flip instantaneously everywhere, so a crew setting out at Putney with a recently changed tide can discover that four miles up-river, the crews emanating from the clubs based there are still experiencing the end of the previous tide. Thankfully, collisions are relatively rare, and happily also for spectators, screaming matches between crews as to who is in the wrong position are much more common.

It gets worse though. There are beaches and sand spits on the Tideway, and from time to time, water flow causes these to change location, height and shape. Thus sculling along minding one's own business confident that one is familiar with the low tide river is not always sufficient. The risk of encountering a new variation of the underlying ground level can sometimes only become apparent when the tearing sound of the boat grounding on gravel disturbs one's concentration. Even should the boat not be physically holed by this excursion, there is every likelihood that the stabilising fin underneath the seat will have been torn off, making for a rollicking row home.

What the Tideway does do, however, is to teach watermanship. Since the conditions in every single rowing outing will differ, extreme care and attentive learning must accompany the focus on hard work and technique. As they say, if you can row and learn your technique on the Tideway, you can do it anywhere. I rowed there at veterans' level for many years. Returning to that narrow Liffey stretch for the first time decades later, I found it hard to believe how benign our little beginner's stretch was by comparison. Probably just as well or I would doubtless have been completely scared off the water for good.

First Coxless Race

But back to Henley in 1976. It's not that by the time of our first race on the Thursday we didn't trust Rory's steering; it was just that we didn't trust Rory's steering. By then I'm not even sure Rory trusted Rory's steering. So we quietly set out some new race rules. We would go off the start at three-quarter pressure; Rory would keep the steering footplate locked in the middle of the boat and not bloody move it; and we would all steer with pressure on the oars.

It worked well. We went off more or less on our racing line and headed off up the course settling immediately into our usual comfortable rhythm. We had to do it on our own though. Our opposition must have spotted some attractive girls on the riverbank because as soon as they were outside the start zone, and hence no longer being at risk of having to contemplate a restart, they drove off at right angles at a decent enough speed. Unhappily, one of the upright stakes must have moved to intercept them because they ran full tilt into it. We never saw them again. I hope the girls concerned were worth it.

Second Coxless Race

This was actually a race in the sense that our opposition survived all the way up the course. Again we were cautious off the start, reckoning that if we came away from the first few strokes in a straight line, we could then safely build the power and the rate and settle into the course. Our caution meant that initially the opposition moved noticeably ahead. I recall, however, being completely unmoved by this, conscious that in a coxless IV there is plenty of scope for sprinting if required later in a race. Happily, here, this wasn't necessary. We sought and found our rhythm, and by a third of the way up the course our bow was in front and we were moving ahead steadily every stroke.

It was some of the sweetest rowing we had done. The boat just seemed to run along effortlessly, and our timing and body movements seemed utterly in synch. Even allowing for the fact that sitting in the 6 seat of an VIII is always going to feel 'heavier' than a lighter coxless skimming along, this was easy, measured and satisfying rowing.

We continued to pull away, and by now Rory was confident enough to move slightly towards the middle of the course, sufficiently to send 'dirty' water, the residual puddles marking where our oars entered and exited the water, down to the other crew, though not so far over as to attract the umpire's attention. Or so he said afterwards when we asked him what the eff he thought he was doing.

Meanwhile, as we were paddling comfortably ahead of the other crew, and had races in the VIII still to come, we concluded that there was no need to contemplate a racing run to the line. The calculations were correct even though the other crew put in a clear sprint as they came towards the end of the course. We came in ahead and continued straight to the landing slips.

The First Quarterfinal

Now we had a problem looming. If we continued to win in the coxless IV, and in parallel in the VIII, the regatta programme would mean four of us having three races on the Saturday, of which two would be semi-finals. This would be grossly unfair to the other four in the VIII and, of course, the reality was that the priority had always been the Ladies Plate.

The next race up was the coxless quarterfinal. After some discussion with Robin, it was agreed that our coxless IV was not to burn itself out. If we got away to a clear and maintainable lead, then well and good. But if we were down significantly, we were instructed not to chase it. The arrangement was that after the first thirty strokes of our start, we could assess what was happening. If we were down, we were not to flog it. This made for an amusing outcome.

We came off the start well but perhaps were a little down. The opposition were throwing everything at it, maintaining a high rate and clearly determined to fight it out all the way down the course. When we hit stroke number thirty we were down but overlapping. Rory called 'steady', which was code for easing the rate but which we also knew on this occasion required us to slacken off the power a little. I said nothing, eased the rate back very slightly as commanded, but kept the power on. I really didn't feel I could back off. I wasn't being noble or sanctimonious about it. I was feeling strong and thought if these other fellows want it, they are going to have to take it. I'm blowed if I'm going to just give it to them.

Then, to my utter astonishment, Dave Weale in the seat behind me said 'fuck 'em, keep the work on' and the pair of us powered away. Rory (who in fairness had a better view being further up the boat) concluded that the other boat was not weakening, and that this would therefore be a more serious race. He called 'steady' again, got no response, and finally lost it and screamed 'back the fuck off, they're well ahead'. The red mist in the stern was dissolving a little by this stage and, conscious that we had another quarterfinal looming, this time in the VIIIs, we duly eased back and settled in to a 'steady state' rhythm.

There are different interpretations of 'steady state' in rowing. Mine has always been to row at 100 per cent pressure but with no adrenaline running, and with a rate per minute in the lower half of the twenties. In other words, hard but not full racing hard. This was also the interpretation of our crew so I allowed the rate to fall off down to about 24, but I could feel that the power was being maintained. In no way was it a soft row, but neither were we going to be gasping at the end.

As we reached the three-quarter mile marker, Weale called out,

'Reilly, I'm bored,' and in truth so was I.

'Me too,' called Richard.

'Okay,' said Rory, 'let's give 'em a fright. We'll build over five, go flat out for 15 and see what happens.'

I started spinning the oar away more quickly from the body immediately at the finish and we built the rate rapidly.

It was as if someone had taken shackles off the boat. It exploded with newfound speed. It was exhilarating. We had nothing to lose even in losing, and it even felt like the boat knew it. Up and up went the rate, darker and darker went the colour of the puddles being pushed away, and we seemed to be going faster and faster every single stroke. I concluded immediately that it mattered not where the opposition was, another 20 or 30 strokes like this and we would row through anyone.

As we shot into the regatta enclosure area several hundred yards before the finish, I could hear the commentator over the Tannoy announcing with clear surprise in his voice 'and Trinity Dublin have raised their rate from 24 to 36!'

All too soon Rory called 'wind down' and this time we obeyed. I glanced over my shoulder to see the opposition stern overlapping with the bow of our boat, and a look of startled fright on the face of their stroke man. As I recall we came in just over a length down. There remains no doubt in our minds that we would have won it had we kept that sprint going, and I recall having no doubt that our speed was rising and not falling as we completed it. For once, however, we had acted responsibly and conserved some energy. As things turned out, we were going to need it.

Meanwhile in the VIII

It was moving well. There were a few nerves in the first race, last year's experience being uppermost in most of our minds. We won it comfortably enough; we won the next round easily; and then came through to take the quarterfinal, again without any real stress. By now the boat was moving faster each race and there was no doubt that the experience in the coxless IV had completely familiarised the stern half of the crew with the Henley water and general racing set-up, and that benefitted the entire crew. Those wins brought up the semi-final and, to our concern, another large American crew loomed into view.

Too Many Trinities

Trinity College, Hartford, located in Connecticut, were (I think) East Coast champions in America that year. Even if I'm wrong in that recollection, they ought to have been. They were enormous, well drilled and ferociously fast. Their size was truly shocking. Biggest of all was my opposite number in their 6 seat. He broke the scales at sixteen and a half stone. And I do mean broke. He sat an exact four stone heavier than me. And they had managed to purloin one of the fastest boats ever used in rowing, the famous Martini Achter used by the US squad in the Montreal Olympics the previous year. It is only famous because it never lost a race. Great.

So here we were again at Henley facing down another bunch of American giants, and these boys had laid down a marker. In the quarterfinal the previous day, they had smashed the course record. I started dreading the race. In fact, I knew several days in advance that we would meet them and I knew it would be horrible.

We studied their times and it became obvious that they were a one speed crew. There was no evidence from their previous races that they started slowly and built up, or that they came out of the blocks quickly and faded. They just seemed to build up to cruising altitude and stay there. I'm not actually sure whether our analysis served any purpose. It was obvious that they were quick, possibly quicker, and certainly more powerful than us. Our best chance was to outrate them in strokes per minute while maintaining every ounce of power which we had, and maybe sprint at the end to catch them napping.

They didn't nap. We were level until the halfway mark and then they started to inch away. Raw power and icy control were their mantras, drilled deeply into them. We did sprint at the end and closed up somewhat, but their power was unrelenting and they took us by a length.

It pulled the lungs out of us. The pain just grew from the halfway point and didn't ever seem to end. By the time we crossed the line it was burning though my chest, and I believe throughout the entire crew. We struggled to get out of the boat at the landing slip. Legs were completely gone. Everyone was white-faced and on the edge of vomiting. I could see most of the crew doing a bum shuffle to exit the boat. None of us could stand up. Despite the fact that our boat had moved really well, we were just simply out-gunned. We were a Hood to their Bismarck. People unfamiliar with rowing on sliding seats don't realise that the legs take most of the strain. Of

The crew coming up to the finish line in the semi-final, with Trinity College Hartford barely a length ahead. Our crew maintained their technique despite the immense and unrelenting pressure at that very late stage of the race. The giant size of the Hartford boys is also readily apparent, especially my opposite number, three seats back from their cox.

course the arms and back do take pressure, but driving the legs off the compressed starting position of each new rowing stroke is when the body puts in maximum effort. The legs are the strongest muscles but nearly 250 rowing strokes at a rate of up to 40 per minute for a sustained six minutes will drain all their power. It's not unlike doing leg squats at a high rate under a decent weight. It saps every ounce of energy.

What was interesting in that race, though, was that we never seemed to lose power, regardless of the stage of the race. We raced them every inch of the way. They broke the course record by six seconds to beat us by a length, which meant we had broken the course record by three seconds. It was actually two outstanding rowing crews, but sadly one was slightly more outstanding than the other. And the other was not actually standing at all by the finish.

Hartford went on the next day to win the final much more comfortably, and in a slower time than their semi-final result. I suppose it was some comfort to us.

There was a little satisfaction for us after Henley, in that we went on to win the Irish Championship that year, and subsequently were selected to represent Ireland at the annual Four Nations race up against England, Scotland and Wales. It wasn't the Ladies, and it wasn't the World Championships, but it was nevertheless a real honour. The green vest is displayed proudly somewhere at the back of my sock drawer.

But would we get another chance at the Ladies?

The crew, with Robin Tamplin in the background, relaxing prior to representing Ireland in the summer of 1976. The fellow fiddling with his hair is the author, with Rory Reilly behind, as ever keeping a watchful eye on him ...

Crossing the River

Sticking with green vests for a moment, two years later I did manage to acquire a second one, this time courtesy of some competitors.

The year I left Trinity, Kieran suggested we should race a pair. We won all of our races, but in truth there wasn't much opposition. Mind you, we would have won them rather more easily if we had avoided walloping each other regularly and focussed instead on improving the rowing. Rowing pairs are worse than an unhappy marriage. I suspect the reason is because you can't roll away from each other when you sense a row developing. In a pair you are stuck within range. You have to stay and fight it out. We did. Regularly.

That year, one of the best Irish clubs, Neptune, had a superb VIII which won everything in its class, and another successful club, Commercial, had four really big and useful oarsmen who also won everything in the smaller boat that same season. As the season drew towards the championships, Kieran and I were approached by Tom Sullivan, one of the most able of the Irish rowing coaches. He was building an VIII around the Commercial IV for one race, namely the Senior Championships, to take on Neptune. He had recruited two of the best Garda Boat Club oarsmen as the stern pair, and wondered whether we might like to jump into the bows? Did Gladys Knight have Pips?

Two days later we were standing outside the Garda boat house. First time for me ever to have stood on the other side of the river. Looking across and downriver to the Trinity Boat House it struck me that was where home had been for the previous four years.

I guess the rest of the crew showed up within an hour of the appointed slot, but to be fair, they were all working, and Kieran and I were idle trainee accountants. We got introduced, launched the boat and clambered in. I had no idea what to expect.

I had never before sat in the 2 seat of an VIII. I couldn't believe the vertical movement up and down and seriously struggled to keep the oar in the water. We got to the top of the navigable part of the river and turned and paddled down. There was a nice rhythm set by M (another man whose name needs to be suppressed for reasons which come later) in the stroke seat, and I seemed to be getting more adept at handling the oar.

By the weir at the lower end of the river we turned again, and in his magnificent gravelly basso profundo voice, Tom shouted across from his bicycle viewing point on the riverbank,

'Ara, we ought to do a few five hundreds.' In other words, short, timed, racing pieces.

M announced to us from the stroke seat what the start would be, but to be honest, I didn't hear a word of it. We sat forward, from the cox's seat Joe Homan yelled 'Go', and the boat took off.

Holy Mother, I had never seen anything so powerful. It was like slamming the Porsche pedal straight to the metal. I dabbed a bit at the water from time to time, praying constantly that I wouldn't crab, and almost immediately came the shout 'wind down'.

God Almighty, the 500 was over already.

'Turn and do another,' came the bellow from Tom on the other side of the river.

I got more of a grip second time around. By the third time, I began to feel part of the crew and realised just how powerful and quick this boat could be. The Championship was a week away.

'What did you think?' I said to Kieran as we headed back to our respective homes to sleep over the accountancy training manuals.

'Jesus, that feckin' thing would have been slower with an outboard engine.'

Seemed to me he was right. More V8 than VIII you might say.

We trained a little in the boat the following week. We also showered and dressed together, but only once. M was in the Garda Special Branch. This unit was largely into counter terrorism so he carried a gun. The Commercial boys hid it the first evening as M was showering after the outing.

Mr. Completely Unflappable lost it utterly when he realised his gun was missing. His reaction was so shocking that the weapon was returned to him immediately. We watched in silence after that, impressed as he donned his Garda motorbike uniform, carefully arranged for the microphone cord to go down from his ear to his wrist, loaded the gun in the holster, mounted the big bike, and went back on anti-terrorist patrol duties. From then on, he arrived and left in his rowing kit. I never before or since saw four grown men look so much like naughty schoolboys every time he appeared thereafter.

We did the last training run two days before the race. Tom said we would do one 500 metre piece only that evening, and that we should throw everything at it. We sat forward and Joe called it.

The boat took off, but instead of blazing away at a typical race start rate of 44 or 46 strokes per minute, and then easing back to 40 or 38, Mick took it off at 42 and held it there. It was a lovely rate with a great rhythm. The boat was really moving rapidly, so easily to me it seemed almost never to be actually in the water. It was as if it were less of a boat and more like some manner of turbocharged water boatman zipping along the surface.

It was an extraordinary piece of rowing. The boat had an inherent speed, requiring almost no effort, and all we had to do was to tap the oars along as if to remind the boat that the speed wasn't to waver. It didn't, it just kept powering along.

Up in the bows, I felt as if I were in a drug-laden speedboat escaping the customs launch. The catches at the start of the stroke were stunningly quick, but perfectly together; the boat balance at all points of the stroke was rock solid; and the strokes were ending with a huge 'send' off the finish which seemed to despatch the swirling puddles away beyond the boat and out of sight. The power seemed limitless and relentless. The hairs on the back of my neck went vertical as we went on and on in the flying 40s. I was in no doubt. This was the fastest crew I had ever sat with.

We came in after the outing and asked, but Tom wouldn't give us the time. He smiled and said I'll tell you on Saturday. I had a growing suspicion that it might, just might, have been the quickest time for a 500 metre sprint that he had ever witnessed. I was pretty certain it was the quickest I had ever experienced.

But how was the fitness? Would these boys last a full 2000 metres? Would Kieran and I, in their company? They had not been pushed all year, winning with comfortable distances in all their races, as had we. The centre four were very big boys, all well over 6 feet, each of them being 15 to 16 stone and maybe even beyond. I was then just about 13 stone and Kieran 14, so to us they seemed gargantuan. But maybe they hadn't really been tested. Could they hold the power for 2000 metres? Could we?

The 1978 Championship Race

We never got to find out. Probably just as well. Lack of rain early in the summer meant that the championship course on Blessington Lake outside Dublin had to be foreshortened to 1700 metres. We were drawn on the extreme left of the four crews in the final. That was fortunate as it meant our stroke man M (then working as an undercover Garda), who was on the conventional side for that seat, could see the other crews without having to turn his head.

Neptune were the real opposition and they were a formidable crew. This was proven beyond all doubt subsequently when, some years later, after Henley Regatta had changed the rules for Ladies Plate entrants, many of the Neptune crew we faced that day went on to win that event. Their talent, fitness and toughness were already evident, however, so everyone in rowing circles expected this to be a ferocious race. It didn't disappoint.

All four crews got away well, and we gradually opened up a lead. It grew steadily and stealthily as we went down the course and at the 1,000 metre mark we had almost a length on Neptune. Both leading crews had by now pulled well away from the remaining pair and it had come down to a straight fight over the remaining 700 metres.

They started to come back at us, stroke by stroke. I could feel the power starting to ebb ever so slightly in front of me, and I wasn't sure mine was going to last the full distance either. We were in that horrible no man's land of the third 500.

M was clearly measuring it very carefully, but for the time being he resisted any urge to make a dramatic rate shift. Joe kept reminding us to keep the power on for every stroke, but still Neptune came on and on, closer and closer. With some 350 metres or so to go they had halved our lead and you could sense that at any moment they were going to launch an almighty charge for the line.

Then M decided to move. Slowly, he pushed the rate up two pips (or strokes per minute), and then another two. The power was now visibly fading throughout our boat but the immaculately timed rate rises sufficed to maintain the half-length lead to the finish.

It was the second Irish championship which Kieran and I had managed to win and, with one exception, it was to be our final race for many years.

The win meant that the crew was automatically select-ed to represent Ireland in the annual Four Nations championship, held that year in Wales. This was actually to be my final race, but only after some petty local politicking had attempted to ease Kieran and me out of the crew in favour of another pair of oarsmen. Oddly enough, we didn't like that particularly, and so offered to race anyone for the spots. That saw them off and we took our rightful place in the fastest boat in Ireland that year.

Sadly in the end, however, some of the boys got a little 'over refreshed' before the race even started and the English VIII came in ahead of us. Nonetheless, a second Irish vest was to be treasured and has again displaced a few socks in the drawer.

Munich

Despite these Irish vests, I never made it to the Olympics. But I did once race with a gold Olympian.

In 2012, I had returned again to rowing, this time with the Masters squad at Tideway Scullers School. (Sometimes rowing is like cigarettes: so easy to give up, time after time.) They were a fit and fast bunch, but when no one was watching I managed to creep into one of the crews at the pointy end of the boat.

In June one year, the squad organiser took a call from four chaps in Bristol. They were a decade older than the IV of which I was then a part, supposedly had wonderful rowing pedigrees, and wanted to know whether we would be interested in joining them to form an VIII for the Veteran or Masters European championships shortly to be held in Munich. We agreed and waited to meet them.

Cultured Oars Coming East

They appeared at Scullers one Saturday morning. They seemed quite serious, if not downright severe, and immediately laid down the law. They would sit in the stern and our four would sit in the bows. Nuts, I thought to myself, how is this going to work? We are younger, fitter and stronger. We should be in the stern, or we should mix it up a little. If we run with their suggestion, unfamiliar rowing styles will split the boat across the middle. For once, however, I stayed schtum, we went out, and to my surprise it wasn't actually too bad at all.

'Shows you what a rowing pedigree means,' said crew member and great friend Tim Sanders, as we came back into the slip after the outing. I think he meant them, not us. Actually, I know he meant them, not us.

I did some research and discovered that there were three Olympians in their four, one of whom, Klaus, had won gold in the German VIII at Rome in 1960, and two others had represented Britain numerous times in the past. Fifty years later, Klaus was trying to collect another winning chunk of metal.

Later in the month, we got to the Munich Olympic rowing course, assembled the boat, did a trial run, and then sat on the bank awaiting our race. At the appropriate time we hopped in, all save for the stroke man who remained standing and addressed us from a great height.

'This is how the race will be run,' he announced.

'The total distance is one thousand metres. The stern four will get the boat into the lead by the five hundred metre mark, and you in the bows will have to keep us there until we get to the finish line.'

I looked at him with barely disguised astonishment. Another packet of nuts I thought. As race plans go, that's the most ridiculous thing I had ever heard. But again I thought I would follow my Mother's advice. Best stay quiet and be thought a fool, rather than open your mouth and remove all doubt.

He climbed into the boat and we paddled up to the start. Awaiting our race, we studied how the starter was handling things. Our time arrived and as we pulled out from the bank towards the stakeboats when disaster struck. The pin holding Klaus' swivelling gate to his rigger suddenly dropped into the water and his oar slid across the boat. No retaining mechanism meant he could not row the oar. Desperately, we hollered to the chap wearing a wet suit in the rescue boat. He came across, dropped into the water and fished around for a time before admitting defeat. No sign of it. Game over I thought.

Klaus had other ideas. Turning to look at me, he yelled out 'go and talk to the control tower' and with that, he slid out of the boat and swam quickly to the bank.

'Why me?' I thought, but nonetheless nodded in agreement. Clambering up the bank, he commandeered a bicycle from one of the nearby watching crew coaches and pedalled off furiously to the boat tents at the end of the course. We got the boat to the bank, and I dutifully clambered out and approached the start control tower.

Climbing to the top of the three flights of stairs, I went into the office to beg the nice *fraulein* to delay our race. She listened politely to my excellent German explanations of the disastrous equipment breakage we had just suffered, the enormous distance we had travelled from England to be here, what a fantastic regatta she had personally organised, how charming everyone had been to us, and would she most kindly hear my pleadings for a delay in the start of our race? After studying me carefully for a minute or two, she grimaced sympathetically, and then told me in impeccable English that the toilet was downstairs. Great.

Meantime the umpire's launch approached the boat and while it wasn't actually cries of *'raus, raus,'* Herr Grumpy in the launch was being quite clear. Get onto the stakeboat now or be disqualified. More pleadings, this time from the crew, some of whom really did speak some German. Most reluctantly, and with a dismissive smirk, he said in essence if you can get unanimous agreement from the other competitors in your race, I will delay ten minutes. Some chance, he clearly thought. The diplomacy commenced, and word was passed from crew to crew across the water. There was unanimous and immediate agreement from every boat comprising five other nationalities. What other sport would do that?

We were surprised and delighted but where the hell was Klaus? Tearing back toward us on the towpath was the answer, clutching a gleaming new replacement pin in his fist. He arrived, meticulously thanked the bike donor, clambered back into the boat and lay back quite exhausted. The pin was passed to the frogman and with help from within the boat the replacement part was bolted in, the oar slotted, and we pulled across to the start.

As we lined up on the start, Herr Grumpy looked at us somewhat surprised and then pretended not to see us at all. I thought, he's bound to disqualify us for something, even if it is only for being too ugly. The stroke man turned around and reminded us of the plan, Grumpy raised the flag and we were off.

I couldn't quite believe what was happening. By the 250 meter mark we were a length up. Good God, I thought, how on earth has this happened? I figured out the answer soon enough. The rate was high to begin with, but it was never brought down. Reality dawned on me. These smarties in our stern had figured out from years of experience that in Veteran or Masters rowing, if you get ahead with some clear water fairly early in the race, everyone else figures that's the race decided, and settles back thinking of the hard work to come in the *bierkeller*. So we flaked along towards the 500 metre marker, out rating everyone but maintaining our one length lead.

The second dose of reality then dawned. The reason the bow four were going to have to bring the boat home was that the boys in the stern were blown up by their rate, as they knew they would be. Bloody hell I thought. After all we have been through getting us to this position, and after Klaus' frantic two kilometre cycle immediately before the race, we can't not win now. There was no sign of the rate being brought down, even if the power in the stern was clearly slipping away. We pulled and pulled in the bow and scraped in by half a length. It was enough.

Afterwards, I felt relieved that Klaus' magnificent solo effort had not been in vain. What a great joy it was for him to return after fifty years and collect another winning medal at the same venue. But also what an exhibition it had all been of the man's determination to achieve it. It struck me that was probably why he had an Olympic gold medal in the first place.

It was of course the height of bad manners to beat the crews which had so decently waited for us. I thought the least we could do was to go and find them and thank them so Tim and I spent the rest of the day in the bar seeking them out. I have no recollection of whether we succeeded.

Year Final

More of the Same? Surely Not

The majority of the Year Two crew had now finished their primary degrees and ordinarily would have moved on to the real world. Richard, in particular, did leave and was much missed. Mind you, he would not have been much missed by the Thames Valley constabulary, responsible for securing the grounds of the Henley Royal Regatta every year, including the year of our semi-final.

Richard, having been well refreshed the evening we lost the semi, was reportedly most indignant to be woken by the police the following morning. After much protesting that they were making rather too much noise with their radios, and had thus disturbed him unnecessarily early on a Monday morning, he reluctantly acknowledged that it was going to be a tad difficult for the police superintendent to concentrate throughout the day if Richard continued to sleep under his desk in their temporary headquarters. He managed to extricate himself to their mutual bemusement, but we heard afterwards that the police woke up somewhat to the realisation that they had a little work to do regarding their own security.

There were three of us with a university year still to complete, and so it was an easy decision for us to decide to row on for another year. The strange thing however was that those who had finished their studies couldn't really let go of thinking about the Ladies Plate. There was by now a general acceptance that we could not have done anything more last year to take the event, but there was also the nagging feeling that we were good enough to take it. It clearly gnawed away at the leavers, and as October rained into November which in turn froze into December, more and more of them drifted back into training.

Problem was, how could they legitimately race for the university having completed their degrees? Start again? The answer soon arrived in the shape of the cheapest primary degree then offered by Trinity, namely Biblical Studies. So they all suddenly became undergraduates again. Somewhat to the amazement of the reverend in charge, and subsequently to his delight, the attendances at his lectures suddenly quintupled, and the average age of his students simultaneously halved.

What surprised everyone however was that, come the year end, it was the big new lumps who came top of the exam results. Mind you, there remains a lingering suspicion amongst the rest of us that an early disclosure by the said lumps to the reverend that they were about to undertake a fact finding mission to the Holy Land over Christmas may well have influenced the year end outcome somewhat. What better way to indicate commitment to the teachings than physically follow in His footsteps. After all, wasn't that straight out of the Holy Book?

Racing on the Suez

Ever since my grandfather had fought in Transjordan (as it was then) under General Allenby in the First War, I had been keen to see Arabia. Arriving at Christmas time from Ireland's dark and grey, damp and short days, Egypt was a different world. The stunning blue sky, the brown sand, the utterly dry air, the unfamiliar noises and smells, but most of all the kaleidoscope of colours, all combined instantly to wash away the northern winter.

On arrival in Cairo, blinking in the harsh light, we were immediately bussed away out to the small town of Ismailia on the west bank of the Suez Canal. What a location. The famous canal glittered as blue as the sky above. Twin sandy banks formed two immaculate straight lines which contained the shrinking blue centre line as it disappeared south as far as the eye could see,

The busy Suez Canal

and the imagination would reach, and beyond. Giant ships made their occasional ponderous way through, looking as incongruous as whales in a bathtub.

It wasn't all beauty though. The Yom Kippur War had ended only three years' previously and passing through the little town there was plenty of evidence of its devastating effect. In particular, our designated hotel seemed to have mislaid the fourth floor referred to in the lift signs. Enquiry revealed that it had been vaporised by an Israeli rocket as their forces headed towards Cairo. Thankfully, all was now peaceful and it was actually very difficult to imagine the noise, damage and death which had existed here, albeit briefly, such a short time ago.

Dave Weale saying 'Hi' from the Suez ferryboat

Canal Rowing

The morning following arrival day, all the crews duly assembled for a few training runs. The rowing equipment being allocated reflected the reality that our sport had not been top of the local post-war rebuilding programme. There was one reasonable VIII, and a sorry collection of other boats which had obviously been uncovered by Howard Carter some half century previously, and left out in the open ever since. Some had seats and some had riggers but never the twain met. In fairness, the local organisers did their very best to make enough complete shells for everyone to get something.

In the end it was decided that the fairest way to allocate the best boat would be to draw ballots. And that's when the true strength of Mr. Topolski's competitive nature emerged. The Oxford legend didn't just win the ballot for the best boat, he also won the ballot for the best oars. And days later when we drew again in Cairo, guess who won everything there also? Even our coach Nick raised an eyebrow at that. And Nick raising an eyebrow was equivalent to the rest of us screaming bloody murder. Well brought up was our Nick.

Actually, we weren't that bothered. Going afloat in Timsah (for Crocodile) Lake, one of the smaller and more shallow of the region's Bitter Lakes, and which borders the town of Ismailia, we were soon paddling out onto the famous canal.

I was in the stroke seat, and could see that Jarlath was concentrating very carefully as we made the right turn out of the lake into the canal proper and set off towards the Red Sea. And then we were out between the sandy sides and I could see the bluest of blue strips of water stretching out behind us as we moved up to a more steady state. It wasn't hard work, which was just as well as we were all just relaxed to be somewhere so warm and sunny. In fact, we were so content to be there, I have no doubt that we would have rowed in a dugout. Come to think of it, that is precisely what we were doing.

We did our training session, got used to the water, tried hard to concentrate and pretty much failed miserably. Given that the last occasion when we had sat in a boat was racing to get here on the cold and wet Blessington lake, it was a simple delight to row in the warmth wearing merely t-shirts while admiring the unfamiliar surroundings.

We raced the following day and Oxford won. *Quelle surprise*. I think we came third overall, but I wasn't really

It's behind you! James, Rory and the author getting curious as to where our dugout was drifting in the Suez Canal

that bothered then and I'm not at all interested now. The fun was only starting, but not in the boats.

Half Cut in a Half Track

The racing over, we headed back to our base, the Hotel De Voyagers, and settled down for dinner. Soon after, the other crews disappeared off to bed, in truth mostly chased there by their coaches who seemed to be playing the role of *in loco parentis*. Actually, as it turned out we were the ones who went loco. We had no interest in early bed, and so quietly ambled over and stood chatting happily at the hotel bar.

Suddenly the door opened, and a big bunch of blue shirts arrived. They were worn by a company of Australians, military fellows deployed on the UN peace line, which was then only a little way out along the road east to Sinai. They seemed delighted to see a bunch of Irish boys and so we all ended up in a group asking them all manner of questions about their lives and experiences. They had money and soon the beers were being poured down us.

Several pints in, one big chap challenged me to a 'knuckle duster'. We put our hands out waist high towards each other with fists clenched pointing down. The aim was to smack the back of the other fellow's hands with your fists before he could pull his away. The Aussie was far smarter and could hold his beer better. My hands started swelling, and as the evening went on I got more and more happy and more and more sore.

Eventually, he took pity on me and seeing the state of my swollen hands, offered me a trip in his halftrack to make up for the damage. I didn't quite believe him, but nonetheless followed him as he left the bar and went out into the warm darkness beyond. I'm quite sure we were both serfectly pober.

And knock me over with a feather (which would have been quite feasible), sure enough there was this enormous, white, semi-tracked open top vehicle parked outside with a big black UN painted on the side. We clambered in and after a sudden roar and lurch into life, the beast set off up the main avenue of Ismailia. It was slow, unbelievably noisy, complicated with levers everywhere, and ever so cool. It was the neatest thing I had ever seen.

'Can you drive?' he asked as he swung the monster around at the top of the avenue.

'Of course,' I lied quickly, watching carefully how he had shifted gears.

'Right then, it's yours.' We swapped places.

I was really concentrating hard. The vision wasn't the best after the unaccustomed volume of beer, but by focussing hard and watching the levers carefully, I managed a couple of gear changes and we set off back down the avenue to the hotel. Then came a loud scraping sound and a shudder on the steering wheel. It didn't feel that big a deal, and I thought I was getting the hang of things fairly well, when the Aussie yelled, 'Stop maite, for chroissakes!'

'Whassamatter?' I protested, 'I can manage the gearbox.'

'It's not that,' he said, 'look up.' Oops. In concentrating on the gearbox, I had taken the steering for granted. I had damn nearly mowed down the first palm tree outside the hotel, and the next in line was looking decidedly nervous. Oh well. Perhaps it might make a comfortable back rest for someone.

A tree outside the hotel with a few of the Cairo Police crew appreciating its Pisa like angle. Wonder how that happened....

Pyramid Romping

We moved on to Cairo. From the quiet, pleasant backwaters of Ismailia, this was the other extreme. Noise, dust, dirt and people, it seemed totally chaotic, and for newcomers it was. But it was exciting. All that movement and smells, colour and action, it knocked An Lar into a cocked fez. Thankfully, the bus driver knew his way to our hotel. He was careful, conscious of that old saying that the most dangerous thing when driving in the Middle East is a green traffic light (because it lulls you into a false sense of security).

We got to our hotel and almost immediately were taken to see the pyramids, just as the sun went down. The bus managed to fit in all the crews and coaches. We had a guide who stood at the front and faced back. She had a tough time. So many comedians making comments at machine gun rates.

'So Cairo has a population problem,' she said.

'We have 8 million people living here, and another 8 million going in and out every day.'

Silence and a laconic American accent drawled out, 'If you've got 8 million people going in and out every day, I'm not at all surprised you have a population problem.' Schoolboy sniggers all round.

The pyramids are genuinely massive. They make the Acropolis look like a little Lego building. We walked all around Giza, paid for the ride on the tourist-hating camels (judging by their spitting and biting attempts), and went off to have supper nearby. The food wasn't the best.

'What is it?' asked Kieran. Chicken, he was told. More like buzzard came his response, and roadkill buzzard at that. It was now dark and we had tickets for the Son et Lumiere show, but it was delayed an hour. I guess after 4,000 years, an hour here or there wasn't going to matter much. A few of us decided we would climb one of the smaller Toblerones, and so walking carefully into the darkness away from the occasional sentries posted at the base precisely to stop stupid tourists from undertaking that very act, we approached the first level of blocks.

Rory, never quite believing that the Sphinx's posterior passage had been truly blocked by the sands of the Nile, deciding to check for himself. At least that's what he said he was doing up there.....

They were about chest high, and with some difficulty we started the climb. The stones were dirty and dusty, it was pitch dark and we ended up separated as we climbed steadily higher.

After a while I stopped and heard scuttling noises near me. What on earth sort of creature lived up here? Ugh. Then voices started up far below me. A bright search-light flared into life and swept up towards me, swiftly followed by a sudden loud gunshot. It was designed to scare the living shit out of us, and in my case it worked precisely as planned. I couldn't move with terror. Was I better off scrambling down as fast as I could, or should I cower here until the sentries went home? I sat as still as the rock behind me, until the scuttling started again. That was it. I slid off down that pyramid like a wet penguin off a mossy rock. I was told later that the scuttling was probably scorpions. Right call, for once.

I think some of the boys may have made it to the top. I never found out. The moment I got to the ground the sound and light show started up. I found a seat and was genuinely impressed, not least by the booming tones of Richard Burton's gravelly voice reciting the relevant history lesson. That fella seemed to have been all over Ancient Egypt, with or without his Cleopatra.

Harvard Training

From the beginning, we mixed with the Harvard boys more than the others. All except Dan and one of the other Oxford boys, the rest kept to themselves, and we got sore necks from looking up at the Washington giants.

Many of the Harvard crew were quite frustrated with their coaches who sent them to bed straight after dinner, before themselves settling down to drinks and rowing war stories. Not only that, but unbelievably it seemed to us, the coaches locked the bedroom doors to ensure no late night flitting could possibly take place. By contrast, and thanks to Nick's relaxed ways, we were allowed to do pretty much as the crew decided. In discussing our various coach's approaches, we mentioned to some of the Harvard lot that, as the Juliet balconies in our Ismailia hotel were quite close together, should they ever wish to slip out, they could always come back in through our rooms, and cross the balconies to their own.

One night they decided to take advantage of our offer, and at about eight in the evening, a group of them appeared on the Trinity balconies, were duly admitted and then slipped out the rear hotel entrance. Given the awful lives they led, we felt it was the least we could do and felt quite magnanimous about it all.

They returned that night after some hours of freedom and tapped quietly at one of our doors. Several of us were inside, including Kieran who wasn't at all well, suffering from a severe head cold. As it happened, when the Yanks entered Weale was sitting holding Kieran's nose, while Rory was slowly pouring some whiskey in to his mouth. The Yanks looked on, stunned.

'What are you guys doing?' they asked.

'Training,' said Rory.

Keeping a perfectly straight face while they looked at each of us in turn was tough, but we managed it.

The Yanks were rich. They had even brought their own food. Stuff like peanut butter was being wolfed down for dinner. We had never heard of it, let alone seen it. But something odd was going on with the Harvard lot. Each mealtime there seemed to be fewer and fewer of them. Eventually, towards the end of the trip there seemed to be literally only one man standing. And what a man. Tall, dark, fit and muscled, we figured him for a Seminole Indian, he was that impressive. What was worse was that he seemed genuinely decent and friendly.

He stopped by our table. 'Any of your guys got the trots?' he asked.

'Nope,' we said.

'Gee, and you are eating the local food?'

'Yup,' said James.

'But how do you sterilise the water?' he asked.

James looked at him for a long minute, then reached under the table and lifted up a bottle of Jameson whiskey.

'We sterilise it with this,' he said.

The Harvard man looked at each of us carefully, nodded in understanding, and slowly headed for bed. Sometimes education can be picked up outside the quadrangle.

Orange Missiles

'Only two piasters?'

'What is only two piasters?' asked Rory.

'A full crate of oranges,' someone said.

'Really? Let's buy one.' And so we did, at the stall by the hotel avenue entrance and headed back up to the bedrooms.

Five or six of us piled into one of the rooms with the oranges. The room was four stories up and looked out across to another wing of the hotel. Down and to the right was the hotel garden, flanked by the entrance to the main road. We started on the oranges and quickly realised that while the top layer was okay, those beneath were hopelessly rotten. 'Swine,' came the politest comment.

We looked out the window, watching Egyptian city life and swearing about the orange seller. Far below, he was packing up for the day. We watched as, wobbling on his heavily laden motorised scooter, he came to a halt at the hotel driveway entrance, waiting for the traffic to ease before leaving for the night.

'Bet you couldn't hit the fecker with an orange,' said Weale.

Rory scooped up a horrible black, orange and brown mess, stood back from the window, aimed and let fly. Smack. Right on the neck. An unbelievable shot. The hand went straight to the neck, the scooter went over, and the man's livelihood rolled down into the gutter, in fairness where most of it belonged. He squealed, shouted and roared with anger, then glared around, and finally started to lift his head to see where the attack had come from. We were far too quick however and were well away from the window by the time his head had swivelled our direction.

The window was, of course, still open. A few minutes later there was a sudden smack on the inside wall opposite said window. We looked at the wall, confused. A horrible dirty brown mess was slowly dribbling down it, and the remains of an orange lay on the floor. A minute later came another, and another and another.

We finally worked it out. The Harvard boys in the wing opposite also had a box of oranges, had seen Rory's missile, spotted us, loaded up their orange missiles with peanut butter, and fired them through our window. What a mess.

Mind you, it didn't take long for Weale to get to the window, yell loudly and point at the Harvard attackers. They laughed at him until they saw the orange seller's glare lock onto their room and he headed straight for the hotel reception. We heard later they got a right chewing out from their coaches and had to cough up compensation to the rotten orange seller. More real world education for Harvard's finest.

Reilly of Arabia trying to count the Pillars with his eyes closed.
You can see from his protruding ribs that he had made the
mistake of sitting by James at mealtimes.

The Cairo Race

This was the high rowing point of the trip, and the truth is I don't recall a thing about it. I recall the river. Big broad and powerful sending a clear message that it was not to be taken for granted. And given the thousands of miles which we knew it had taken to reach us, we were pretty respectful of it.

I do recall coming ashore after the race though and trying to clamber up onto the floating pontoons which rose and fell alarmingly with the wakes of passing commercial craft. Fortunately, we were boating out of the Arab Contractor's base, and there could not have been a more helpful bunch of fellows determined to ensure that none of their guests went for an unexpected swim.

And then we returned to the hotel to attend some flash ball or other being held in our honour, but I have bored you already with that event.

Dinner with the Tourags

All the other crews and half of our squad set off home the following morning. They did have to make two attempts to leave Cairo though. First time around, one of the EgyptAir engines got tired and went for an immediate kip, and so the airplane circled off Alexandria dumping fuel for a couple of hours. This rather confused Weale somewhat as, immediately on boarding, he had settled off to a deep sleep. He hadn't had much of it the previous night, what with having discovered how much he enjoyed the single malts in Shepheard's Hotel and all.

Waking as the plane landed back in Cairo he wondered aloud how it was that the January weather in London was so much better than Dublin's finest offerings in the dead of winter.

When the plane came to a stop, however, his wonderment ceased as he, along with everyone else, was required to zip down an emergency chute and quickly realised that he had gone precisely nowhere. He was quite calm about it all, in stark contrast to the wife of one of the American coaches, whose husband was heard to mutter ungraciously as they stood on the hot tarmac:

'Shoot, Wendy's just gone and fudged her knickers.'

Poor Wendy. Having to go commando all the way back to Washington state. I do hope she didn't catch cold.

As for the rest of our gang, we decided that we would like to see Luxor and Aswan, the latter being the famous triptych site of the High Dam, Hercule Ustinov's Cataract Hotel, and the Temple of Philae. Oxford's Dave Thompson didn't get to race as he was the spare cover for their crew, but very sportingly he volunteered to accompany us. He went off and bought the train tickets for all of us from Cairo. They cost the grand sum of two local pounds each, but it did take him all day to secure them.

So that same evening, we boarded the train, headed unthinkingly and unknowingly into third class, and were pleasantly surprised to be ushered forward by the locals. Not that there was much choice, what with most of the seats enjoying double occupancy. In fact, there seemed to be no seats available anywhere until we got to the sleeping carriages. These cabins appeared empty and so James took charge, chose one, we settled in, and he carefully locked the door behind us and affixed the security chain.

All went well for a few hours until a commotion started outside. We held our nerve and ignored the demands to open the door. Suddenly the lock spun around and the door opened as far as the chain allowed. We smiled confidently until with a sudden bang it gave way and the guard, with a soldier attached, arrived in.

All in all it was getting a bit crowded and I was minded to complain somewhat. Meanwhile, the soldier had his rifle with him, but I suspect not even this would have stopped James from exiting the fresh entrants, had Nick not pointed out to him that the rifle was, quite unsportingly we thought, pointed at a spot a few inches below his waist.

The Temple at Aswan
(photo by Warren LeMay, Wikiepedia Commons)

So we stood in the corridor. Or tried to stand. It is pretty much a straight line south from Cairo to Luxor, but some comedian had built in a chicane every few hundred yards, or so it felt. The train seemed to sway alarmingly through them, tossing us from one side of the corridor to the other. After a time Nick voiced what we were all feeling, namely that we were not going to be able to stand there for much longer.

It was getting late but it was also becoming clear that we were not going to be able to sleep on the narrow corridor without being trampled underfoot by the staff and other passengers. Depressed, we trudged forward standing aside from time to time as well fed passengers came against us, the dining room then closing. Maybe we could buy a dinner between us and make it last six hours?

We got as far as the dining room to be told dinner was finished. We spied oodles of sleeping room beneath the tables. The purser caught our glances and proposed money should change hands. This would have been a good outcome, had we had any. Suddenly he looked at me and said 'aspirin'. I twigged and drew out a packet from the communal medical kit. Big smiles all around and we drew out the sleeping bags, the lights went out, and we stretched out under the tables. At last. Bliss.

Some hours later a sudden high pitched screeching sound erupted, the train lost all its speed and, inter alia, we were all sent rolling along under the tables until we banged up against each other, and the table legs. The train stopped and there was total silence. The lights went on and harsh voices sounded at the end of the carriage. We watched transfixed, but surreptitiously, as the purser ran to the end of the carriage, and then appeared to walk

The author, just checking that coach Nick Tinne had the money for the Aswan ferry, while James tries not to drop his sandwich in the sands of the Nile

backwards towards the front, chattering quickly. He was followed by four sets of large, black-clad legs ensconced in what seemed to be World War I army boots. We lay still.

After a very short time we smelt dinner, and I took a peek. Four of the largest men I had ever seen, dressed head to toe in black. Skin so dark it was cobalt blue under jet black headdresses. As I looked more carefully I saw one rifle and what looked like seriously large sword blades sitting on the table. Wilkinson's they were not, by any stretch of the imagination. I slid carefully back down and motioned silence to the boys. A little while later the big boys got to their feet and strode out of the car.

Soon the lights went out and the train restarted. I don't think they caught sight of us from start to finish, and I thought on balance we could live with that. Mind you, I quite fancied a jet black *djellaba*. I figured it might make me look bigger and meaner.

We heard next morning that they had stopped the train with burning logs placed across the tracks. Clearly easier and quicker than buying tickets, and dinner came free.

We loved Luxor. Stunning, beaten only by the next town on the way up river.

No Deaths on the Nile

Aswan is even more stunning. Go there. It is better even than the films depict it. Clear blue skies parked above the equally blue ribbon of life, overlooked on the dead (west) side by gentle green and sandy hills dropping right down to the river. On the hill opposite the town sits a perfectly formed baby fort, which we discovered is the designated final resting place of the Aga Khan, leader of the Ismailian sect of Muslim believers. Inside it is open to the sky.

A very elderly retainer sat outside when we arrived at the entrance. He was dressed in matching immaculate white long sleeves and legs, and positioned to ensure that all were respectively attired before being allowed in. A model of grace and calmness, but clearly taking his responsibilities seriously. We were happy to oblige. It was impossible not to be struck by the serenity of the entire location.

Down below, the little feluccas with their immaculate white sails drifted up and down the smooth flowing river, as they ferried people, goods and animals from one side to the other. We explored the area, intrigued by the unfamiliar items on sale in the little souk ('Tutankhamun's ring for very good price'), while simultaneously taken aback by the subsistence living being endured by most of the people.

One shop just sold oranges and their juice. A tiny bakery sold two types of loaves. The little vegetable shop sold a few tomatoes, a few potatoes and twenty varieties of dates. And everywhere, cheeky little urchins were offering to help guide us around. And everywhere, but everywhere, despite the grinding poverty, everybody smiled.

Can one be content with nothing? Could this ancient race, having known 'civilisation' before the word was ever written in the West, have evolved away from chasing the material life that we so hungered after? Or was it that there was no choice but to make the best of what they had? But if the latter, why all the smiles? You never get a smile from a man driving a Rolls Royce.

We never did figure it out.

Years later I can still picture the scene and promise myself to get back there. Meanwhile, we reluctantly gave up our warm sojourn and philosophical enquiry, and headed back north to settle uncomfortably back into the dark and drizzly January days, our version of civilisation.

A Different Sort of Ladies

Girls didn't really row much then in Ireland. Personally, I hadn't given it a thought beyond the fact that I wasn't really meeting any girls and wondered whether that would ever change. Then a girl called Jane Williams arrived into Trinity and decided to change all that. Her then boyfriend (and thereafter husband) was Dave Sanfey. Dublin University Ladies Boat Club had just been formed.

Jane procured a boat and a few crews of girls, and immediately the club changed utterly, and for the better. There was some opposition. Some of the men felt that the girls would compete for the annual capital grant from Trinity required to keep the men's fleet competitive. So to avoid any overt squabbling, the decision was taken that the two sexes would keep their respective distances. It worked really well as a policy. Out of the Trinity men's first VIII, only three of us married members of the Ladies Boat Club. A ratio of 33 per cent. So much for a policy of keeping distance. It might have worked during daylight hours but Ireland is quite dark for a lot of months in winter. In reality, of course, it did work very well for the three men and, one hopes, the girls concerned. Maybe the Boat Club constituted a bonus 'target rich environment' for the university sorority who had already decided to row?

In April of Year Final, I was standing on the boat slip, prior to heading off for the day, the VIII outing having finished. A four oar boat approached and as I looked I could see that it was going to miss its landing. I called out, grabbed an oar as it passed, and hauled the boat to the slip. It was a girls' crew and the girl on the other end of the oar looked up and smiled at me. I almost fell in the water. Such a smile. Such eyes. Finding all manner of daft irrelevant reasons to continue hanging around like some dopey drone around the hive, I could not take my eyes off her. Who on earth was she, and when had she appeared?

'She' was Jane Johnston who had joined the Ladies club with no rowing experience and had stepped straight into the top crew. An absolute rowing natural. Over the succeeding weeks I contrived to bump into her anywhere and everywhere, but since she was a microbiologist and I was a mere miserable economist, there wasn't any academic overlap. I did, however, manage to spot her at the Boat House on occasion and refined the drone routine.

I had two immediate wishes. The first was that she would turn out not to have a serious boyfriend. After some weeks, that turned out to be the case. The second was that she would have absolutely no taste whatsoever when it came to men. That way I would have a chance. And actually, that worked out as well.

After a regatta later that month I enquired whether she might be going to the disco that evening in Commercial Rowing Club, and could scarcely believe my luck when she said yes. The following Saturday both clubs were heading to Castlewellan just over the Northern Ireland border for the island-wide university championships, and the men's and women's clubs were to share a coach.

I must have been at the coach park an hour before the thing arrived, so desperate was I to secure a seat towards the front of it, hoping to entice her to sit with me. It worked a charm despite having to boot out most of my own crew who automatically plonked themselves beside me without any thought, as they spied the empty seat. At length she arrived, we chatted there and back, and haven't really stopped since.

At the time, however, and given the background, both of us felt it might be diplomatic to keep the burgeoning relationship very quiet. This worked well. Sometimes too well. Later in May, we became aware that we had both been invited to the same party at someone's house on the Saturday night.

That Party

I wasn't really a party fellow and as the hour approached I regretted suggesting to Jane that I would see her there. I really wanted to see her but going to a party where everyone else would be rat-arsed with alcohol while I was stuck in dry training didn't appeal much.

Nonetheless, because I was keen to see her, I went along and for a couple of hours stood and listened to the usual intense but irrelevant rantings of drunken students. Because the men's and ladies' clubs weren't supposed to be intermingling, Jane and I thought it best if we at least arrived separately and didn't spend the entire evening together. I spotted her when I got there, but she was engrossed with her mates so I hung back.

And then the host appeared at my elbow and said,

'Dave, come and talk to the lads,' meaning some classmates, so I allowed myself to be steered across the room.

Just as I got there, Jane materialised saying 'Hi' to one of the other fellows and then to our host. He suddenly had a brainwave and out of the blue said to me, 'Dave, I'd like to introduce you to Jane Johnston. Jane this is Dave, he's a rower.'

Jane kept a beautiful straight face, as did I (but without the beauty), and we each voiced the usual mush;

'Hi.'

'How do you know our host?'

'What are you studying?'

Yadi, yadi, yadi, yawn, yawn, yawn …

Now, meanwhile, I was having a technical problem in the boat. John at stroke was physically shorter than me by a good few inches. With a very fast catch at the start of the stroke, and with his oar moving through the stroke like an uncoiling whiplash, he was fast out of the water at the finish. I noticed that with serious concentration I could get in at the catch at the same time, but without committing the cardinal sin of rowing, namely, shortening up on the length of the stroke, I simply could not get out of the water at the same time.

I thought I would confide to someone and approached Weale to explain my problem.

'Aw, man, like it's cool, okay, totally cool. Take some weed.'

Shit. I hadn't realised that he was no longer our Baby East German but had now moved from Leipzig to Laurel Canyon. Great.

I got more sense from Rory.

'We're talking milli fractions Dave, but I have exactly the same problem, and I'm guessing so has the rest of the boat. You and I should ensure that we both exit the stroke at exactly the same time, and the rest of the crew will follow us since I'm in the 7 seat, you're in the 6 seat and so all the crew will see one of us. If we are together the crew will finish each stroke at the same time. After all, we really only need John for the first half of the stroke and to keep us slow on the slide. To make sure we are together, on the next piece of work, let's both put an extra 5 per cent on to the finish and spin out clean and together.'

Or something like that. I can't remember exactly, but there was some technical issue around that we were trying to fix.

Whatever it was, we tried it for the last piece of work on that morning's outing. It seemed to work. I started to feel more comfortable, the timing of the finish generally seemed to coalesce better, and the boat seemed more comfortable. But I was keen to see whether we could repeat it from the first strokes in the next morning's outing, and was therefore keen to get home for some sleep (well that's my story and I'm sticking to it). But before that, back to the frightful party…

The others joined in the chat with Jane and me, and then I simply ran out of patience. Unusual for me, as I am blessed with immense patience, exceeded only by the self-delusion. So I looked at the host and said:

'I'm really sorry but I have an early start, would you mind if I slip away early?'

'No, of course not, you rowers need your beauty sleep,' came the patronising response, which served only to piss me off even more. So I dropped all pretence.

'Jane, do fancy coming home with me? My rooms are in college.' The others looked up and smirked.

Jane thought about it for a moment, and keeping a perfectly straight face said quite evenly, 'Sure, why not.'

Well the next sound was all the jaws hitting the floor as the rest of them gaped at the two of us. They were still gaping as we smiled our goodbyes and headed out.

For the rest of that term, our host became the biggest recruiter of future rowers the Boat Club ever had.

'Wow, you should see the way these rowers attract the girls…'

I hope he never gets to read this.

A Wedding (Feast of Troubles)

Notwithstanding that party, Jane and I stayed together. Accordingly, some years later, like a good (by then qualified) accountant, I got married on a date which was a numeric palindrome, 28/8/82. The date is all the more memorable, given the events leading up to it.

I was never favoured by my prospective father-in-law (PIFFLE for short), in fairness for three very sound reasons:

1. I was not a rugby player and he couldn't see why his eldest daughter would not choose to marry someone in a sport he loved. He thought there was plenty of choice amongst the Irish rugby squad, and failed utterly to understand why Jane didn't fancy a front row thug with a squashed nose, mangled ears, a waddling gait, and weighing near twenty stone. Pretty boy rowers didn't do it for him.

2. I was a Southern Mick or 'Free Stater' and his family were stout Northern Protestants, and to cap it all,

3. I was far too bloody cheeky.

Move along now Jane, nothing to see there... In due course over the subsequent decades he and I did develop a very solid relationship. I slipped easily into Stupid Boy role to his Cap'n Mainwaring commanding presence. Mind you, initially I have to admit, he did have some grounds for his long held opinion.

The night before the wedding, he and my (lovely, sweet) prospective mother-in-law hosted a dinner at the fine hotel they owned on the north side of Dublin Bay, for all the wedding principals (as distinct from principles – there were few if any of those left by then).

Someone was deep into regaling a story about some idiot who set off on his honeymoon minus his passport when PIFFLE noticed the stricken features of his prospective son-in-law. The table gradually felt silent as he continued to look unwaveringly at me until finally he growled:

'You have, haven't you?'

I closed my eyes and nodded my head.

'In London?'

I nodded again.

'Ye gods,' he announced to Jane, 'you're marrying a nodding donkey but with less brains.'

There wasn't really much of a comeback to that one.

Thankfully, my brother Howard (easily the smartest of all us siblings) sorted it. Overnight he got his flatmate in London to drive to our next door neighbours' Wimbledon house; convinced them to allow him access to our house using their emergency set of keys; identified the right sock drawer holding the precious item (it is always just beside the Irish vests for any aspiring thieves reading this); drove to Heathrow airport; and there convinced an Aer Lingus pilot to bring the passport to Dublin Airport from where another friend collected it. It was delivered into my hand at the wedding breakfast. And all in the days when there were no mobile phones. A narrow escape as the honeymoon was scheduled to start in France the day after the wedding.

Almost the Best Man

In deciding who to have as best man, Kieran was last out of the room and kindly stepped up. It was a dangerous appointment for both of us as we still bore the scars (physical and mental) from our less than fraternal year rowing in the pair.

Now Kieran is one of the kindest and most considerate people one can ever hope to meet, but sometimes there is so much kindness and consideration being doled out that there remains no space for the concept of time. I was therefore scrupulous about anticipating every possible problem which could delay us on the morning of the wedding, and meticulously lied to him about the starting time of every aspect of it.

In the week leading up to the wedding, Kieran was driving his late father's fine big Mercedes. The perfect vehicle in which to be chauffeured to one's wedding, I thought. As the week progressed, however, I noticed that the left rear tyre was slowly deflating. I probably only mentioned it in passing to Kieran ten or twenty times over the space of a few days.

'Fuck's sake, remember to change that wheel.'

'Woudja ever fuck off, of course I'll fukkin' change the fukkin' wheel,' was the politest exchange on the topic.

More evidence of a pair of finely educated young gentlemen, masters of wit and repartee.

Come collection time the morning of the wedding, Kieran marched into my parents' house, greeted everyone cordially with his great big smile, complimented my Mother on her outfit (he was such a crawler) and carefully saw everyone out of the house before slamming the front door behind us all.

Even more decently he then made sure that everyone set off safely in all the various cars to drive to the church, some ten miles away up the coast road. Only then did he unlock the Mercedes allowing me to sink with relief into the comfortable armchair of the front passenger seat.

I suppose I was comfortable for all of five yards. Barely had the car set off when it became bindingly obvious that there was a problem, and we both simultaneously knew it was the left rear tyre.

'I don't want to hear it,' was the first comment.

As I was speechless with fury, it could only have come from him.

When my voice returned I simply growled, 'I'm not marrying Jane with oil and grease all over my mitts. Your car, your problem,' I said menacingly.

'No problem, calm down, oodles of time,' came the response.

I watched (I have to admit impressed) as he smoothly opened the boot, removed the jack, expertly slid it under, quickly raised the car, deftly spun the wheel nuts, whipped off the wheel, hoiked out the spare from the boot, whipped the nuts back on, chucked the left rear into the boot and, with a flourish, hit the jack and watched the car drop back down. All the way to the rim of the spare wheel which by then was making the average pancake look somewhat plump. Flat, flat, flat. Shit, shit, shit.

'Where's your car?' he enquired aggressively.

'In the garage behind the house. You know the house over there to which we don't have any keys, and from which you saw everyone off to the wedding that isn't going to happen? That one.'

We set off down the adjacent laneway, round the back of the house, and up to the back doors of the garage.

'Over you go,' he said.

I yelled, 'Whaaaat? Wearing a full morning suit?'

'Prefer a ten mile hike in it do we?' he snapped back. No option.

I clambered up onto his knee, then his shoulder and, resisting the temptation royally to kick his head in, I struggled up onto the garage roof at the end of the garden, praying that Dad's cheap rusty galvanised strips would hold. They did. Just. But the swaying had me feeling seasick. The morning was really getting worse by the minute. I got down the other side and then, just like George Peppard always said it would in the A Team, the plan came together.

My former bedroom window faced the back garden, and an elderly lean-to shed was under it. I was praying that my youngest brother Andrew had not changed his habits from years previously when I was living there. Being on the verge of a professional cycling career, he never took alcohol save when granted a training break. When allowed, however, he and his mates really hit the stuff.

I prayed further that last night had been such an occasion and that therefore my bedroom window would be unlocked. He was usually so pissed, it was all he could do to crawl down the corridor to his room without waking the household. Lock my window after him? He never even closed the bloody thing. Mother never knew why I was always looking for another blanket come wintertime. Sure enough, it was open, I clambered in, found the keys to my car, reversed my steps and was soon opening the garage doors.

My car in those days was a sporty red Lancia Fulvia, which for its time was quite quick. It needed to be. We were now seriously late. We set off down the hill and turned left on to the coast road. I was still speechless with rage. Kieran (with his usual surprisingly high emotional intelligence) clearly reckoned he was in serious danger of being slung out once I hit the 60 miles per hour mark, so cleverly decided to change the subject.

'I need to put some cash into the envelopes for the two variations on the clergy theme (it was what was known then in Ireland as a 'mixed' or two religion wedding), the flower person, the choir and choirmaster…' The litany (!) went on.

Still in a barely contained fury, I barked out numbers and Kieran dutifully pulled out lumps of the folding stuff, squashed them into the envelopes, and scrawled names on the outside.

'Oh,' he then said, 'I've forgotten the organist, how much shall I give him?'

I looked across, scarcely able to believe we were doing all this at this late stage. 'Why not wait until we hear how he plays?' I said savagely.

He laughed and actually even I thought it was quite a good line, until I heard it again three hours later when he recounted the conversation as part of the best man's speech in the presence of the organist, who immediately but furtively pulled out said envelope to see what the jury had decided upon.

As it happened he did rather well, having weaved the Eton Boating Song into his musical nurdling before the arriving Queen of Sheba took over his organ (as you might say), while Jane and PIFFLE came up the aisle.

But meanwhile I had my foot to the floor. Racing north out along the coast road meant that there was no danger of traffic coming from my right. There were few enough other cars about, and so as I came to the various traffic lights, I was able to move illegally to the wrong side of the road, ignore their colour, and keep my foot down.

This worked well for the first five miles but it was then I noticed a motorcycle Garda settling in behind us. I was travelling at 70 in the 40 zone. I really didn't care. I had a clear choice. Slow down and listen later to PIFFLE holding me to account for being late for his daughter's wedding, or keep the foot down and listen to some pontificating magistrate wittering on about speed limits. No contest.

I held the speed for about another mile, at which point the siren started howling and the blue light blazed on and off. No choice now. I slowed and stopped. He came up to the window still astride his machine and looked in. I lowered the window.

'And where might you two be going at that speed this hour of the morning?' looking carefully at two men in morning suits at 5 minutes to 11 o'clock on a Saturday. Clearly no detective promotion coming his way in the foreseeable future.

Finally, finally, the pressure got to Kieran. I had been starting to admire his calmness under my fire but was now delighted to see the edifice developing a structural crack.

'Ah now Sergeant, this fella is terrible late for his weddin', couldjya just let us go for the love of Jesus, Mary and Joseph?' Bless.

Well would you believe it, it worked. 'Go on,' he said.

I decided to push our luck. 'Any chance of an escort?'

Kieran put his head in his hands.

The Garda laughed. 'Jayzus, lads I would, but I don't think I could keep up. Get on with yez.'

We passed Jane and PIFFLE in their classic Lanchester wedding car a mile from the church as it cruised languidly towards my on again marriage. We were probably travelling some 50 miles an hour faster than the old vintage motor. I doubt they ever saw us.

I have no memory of driving up the church avenue, but years later when Jane and I went back there for auld times' sake, mention was made of a collection to fund the replacement of all the gravel. It seemed that years back it had all been scattered by some lout driving far too quick-

A white-faced groom with his new bride, his pallor hardly surprising given the antics on the way there. On oar duty and framing the young couple are from left, Jim Jackson, James Murnane, Rory Reilly and His Honour Judge Donagh J MacDonagh. Overseeing from the rear is Kieran Mulcahy, a forced smile disguising his regret at ever having agreed to act as Best Man.

ly in such a confined space. It was a clever comment from a clever clergyman with a good memory and a broad smile. I realised I had little option but to empty my wallet into his collection box. I suppose that what was meant by the sign at the end of the church avenue, 'Jesus saves'.

Nottingham and Durham

The 1976/77 academic year had gone past in a blur. The racing season came round so quickly it was hard to believe that yet again we were lining up for Henley. There was no doubt about this campaign, however, it would be the final attempt by this crew. There was only so much of the Old Testament that a fella could take. Again, we took in the Nottingham regatta en route.

We looked around at Nottingham for the opposition, being somewhat fearful of giant Americans, but didn't notice any crew that seemingly spelled trouble. And feeling quite comfortable, and with the boat moving well within the targeted times for the set practice distances of 500 and 1,000 metres, we looked forward to the final. We knew it would confirm our superiority.

Did it hell. We had a rotten row. No rhythm, too much rushing, all of us desperately trying to lever forward a boat seemingly stuck in Grandma's treacle pudding, and refusing to play. We got beat. We could not bloody believe it. A crew from Durham University had come in ahead of us. Who the hell were they and where had they come from (other than Durham obviously)? What was worse, we discovered that they were lining up confidently for the Ladies Plate at Henley the following week. Not again.

Slugging It Out to Henley

Depressed, we grumpily loaded the boats, snapping and snarling at each other like a bunch of mangy dogs squabbling over an empty fish and chips bag. By the time we had found somewhere to eat and munched our way silently through supper, it was fully dark when we set off down the motorway heading for Henley.

Earlier that year Rory had purchased a green Morris Minor. Similarly, Kieran had purchased one of British Leyland's finest (an oxymoron if ever there was one), a red Morris 1100. If Rory's car was christened the 'Galloping Maggot', then Kieran's version had to be the 'Red Slug'. It was horrible. But at least you could find it easily in the car park. Just follow the trail of oil and at the end you would find the car arranging its next union strike.

Rory really had been quite naughty and selected the two lightest men in the boat to travel with him. James was in his supportive parents' car, which left the remaining five, including me, to go with Kieran. The Red Slug amply lived down to its nickname. Half an hour south on the M1, with most (maybe all) of its contents fast asleep, it decided to blow out a front tyre. We knew it was a front tyre because the car spun in a complete circle, bashed all heads awake against the windows, and finished up facing north in the middle lane.

There were very few cars about so the fairground bumpers game never really got going. One chap did stop, confused by the headlights facing him, and offered to help. Meanwhile, we clambered out, found the spare and quickly joined its deflated state (what *is* it about Kieran and flat tyres?). The Samaritan drove off to a services, filled the spare with air, somehow found us again, and two hours later we set off once more.

Obviously, we had stayed twice before at Henley, but luckily everyone forgot to make the usual booking this year, and so at the very last minute coach Rob Van Mesdag called the Regatta Stewards who, at short notice, very decently lined us up to stay with the local GP and his wife, Terry and Elaine Dudeney, and their delightful two children. It was their first year of hosting a rowing crew. We got there in the small hours and crept quietly to bed.

Breakfast came as something of a shock to Doc Terry. A scruffy bunch of large men materialised, introducing themselves after a muttering fashion, all the while looking forlornly at the single box of Rice Krispies on the table. Kieran did his usual diplomatic act and went straight for the kitchen to charm Elaine. He emerged holding a mixing bowl and pint of milk, emptied half the cereal packet and all the milk into the bowl, and went to work. Doc Terry's face fell as he quickly started to recast his expected food bills.

Elaine rescued everyone by suddenly producing biblical quantities of bread and eggs. Terry thought it would be polite to talk, and so his starter for ten was,

'So, how do you think you might do at our regatta?'

Coming off the previous day, we were all trying not to think about it. Of course, we all knew what the mission was, and what therefore the only possible response would be, but it was left to the boat leader, John, to voice it.

*Scruffy lot after a Henley training run in 1977. Mind you, the
timing looks reasonable on bow side. For once. From the left,
Slimmed down Jarlath, Afro John, Farmer Reilly, Sweaty Author,
Gasping Weale, Posing James, Naked Sanfey, Mexican Ted,
Curious Kieran and a little bird pacing us.*

'We better effen win it,' he said, and went back to the
nosebag. Had we looked up we would have seen Doc
Terry's look of disbelief. It lasted fully three days until
our first race.

Focus

They were a great band in the 1970s, but there was
a different kind of focus around with us. Robin
exemplified it. His concentration could be so intense that,
on occasion, he seemed to be utterly oblivious to the rest
of the world.

He was concerned that our starts were not quite fast enough, and so he sought out some crews against which he wanted to match us. One such that year was the men's GB quad. A quad, four men with two sculling oars each, is usually the fastest boat away from a standing start, so Robin figured if we could practice holding off these fellows we might polish up nicely.

So we lined up at the start of the course, Robin aimed his bicycle up the towpath to follow us and take stroke ratings, someone shouted, and we took off for thirty strokes. The quad immediately took a man, and then another and another until their stern was level with me in the 6 seat. But then it didn't move any further in front while we held the high rate just that bit longer than usual. Jarlath's commanding voice over the speaker said, 'wind down' and we eased the rate and power right off.

The Wet Tandem

Heart rate heading back down, I looked across to my right to see Robin's reaction. I couldn't tell. He was totally focussed on the stroke watch, which would have given him the number of our strokes per minute as he pedalled along. Something moved at the corner of my eye and I turned my head further. Flying down river was an American crew with a coach following on the towpath. He was not alone. As I looked more carefully, I could see that the coach was on the rear of a tandem bike and in front was what I assumed was the spare man for the crew, who was head down, pedalling furiously.

I glanced back at Robin and my gaze froze. He was still focussed on the watch and to my horror I saw now that both bicycles were about to meet at the narrow pedestrian bridge where the towpath hopped over a small stream joining the main river. I knew there to be barely room for two people to pass, or one bicycle. There was nothing I could do except close my eyes and wish him the best of luck.

There came an almighty splash followed by a bellow of rage, and gingerly I looked up. Robin was still on the bike, had passed the bridge and unbelievably was still focussed on the watch. The rear wheel of the tandem was sticking out of the water and two furious Americans were trying to work out what on earth had just happened, as they scrambled for the riverbank. I kept quiet lest they identify that somehow their nemesis was connected to our boat, wearing as it was its racing number.

After the outing I asked Robin whether he noticed anything after our start, and he said he did.

'The stroke watch seems to be playing up; I'm afraid I didn't get your rating, but it looked high…'

Bless him.

Coaching does mean serious concentration, however, which means that if the crew are not contributing to this, things can get frustrating. Years later, and on a voluntary basis, I was helping out with coaching the 16-year-old crews of a local school. Jarlath was staying overnight with me, and in a foolish attempt to shake off the previous evening's wine consumption, I invited him to cycle with me on the Sunday morning to look after a one of the crews.

Unfortunately, the crew I allocated to him had a whining kid aboard. Accompanying the crew, Jarlath cycled from below Kingston Bridge to Hampton Court Palace and back. This didn't really ease the hangover and I could tell he was far from amused about being out and about so early. I felt for him as, despite being some distance away watching another crew, I could hear the constant moaning emanating as Jarlath's crew wound all its way up and then down the four-mile stretch of otherwise peaceful water.

On the return, crossing a busy Kingston Bridge on his bike and having suffered this bleating for over an hour, Jarlath looked down on the crew as it passed under and finally snapped.

'Stop,' he yelled, and the boat obliged.

'Are you ever going to shut the eff up,' he roared at the offending youth.

'But Sir, it hurts,' came the whingeing response.

Silence before Jarlath finally bellowed back:

'Sonny, rowing is like sex. If it hurts, you're doing it wrong.'

Overhearing this, I saw the rest of his crew, and all the other boats, lapping up the 'wisdom' and everyone rowed happily away, even the moaning minnie. As expected, however, there were complaints received by the school on Monday morning from offended onlookers (who seem to be everywhere these days) for the 'lewd language' used, allegedly by one of the school masters. After making due and careful enquiry, the headmaster was able confidently to confirm to all the complainants that the school had no rowing masters overseeing the outing that morning, and hence they should look elsewhere for the culprits.

There can be the occasional real coaching frustration. In the main, there are no 'touchline Dads' attempting to visit their own failed sporting ambitions on the lives of their offspring in our sport. The touchlines can be a tad damp. It did happen to me once however. Again helping out at the same local school, I was asked by the head of rowing to look at a particular crew shortly before the regatta season. He felt that while the crew was fit, strong and technically adept, it did not seem to be rowing to its potential speed. I went out with the four boys one summer evening, and observed them as they went through their allotted work pieces.

At length I concluded that the rhythm might be the problem. Summoning them back in to the landing slip, I swapped the stroke man out of his seat (quickly telling him he was needed for the 2 seat, and so remembering my lesson from Mr. George's class), and installed the 2 man in his place. The crew went back out for a short outing and having returned, immediately confirmed that the new combination seemed to work much better and suggested that we keep it that way for the season. None of us, however, reckoned on the former stroke man's father intervening.

'What's all this then?' came a loud voice as the crew sat in the boat at the slip before disembarking.

I turned around to see an aggressive looking man addressing me. 'What's all what?' I said.

'My son is the stroke of this crew and who do you think you are taking him out of that seat?'

I tried the reasonable approach. 'I think the boat runs better in this combination'.

'I don't give a flying fuck what you think, whoever you are, my son stays in the stroke seat. Is that clear?'

It certainly was, but to be honest, I really didn't care. I wasn't coaching that crew and had no vested interest in its performance. I wasn't interested in some daft row with a misguided parent. I simply smiled at him and said:

'Fine by me mate. Perhaps you'd like to coach the crew instead? Have you done much rowing?'

'Don't get fucking smart with me.'

Again I wasn't bothered. I had helped out at the request of a friend. I didn't need the grief. There was a tragedy developing, however, and I saw it in the eyes of the lad I had moved to the 2 seat. There were tears welling in his eyes as he sat there looking mortified.

Supporting your child is usually the right and proper thing. Abusing someone who is assisting your child in their growing endeavours, however, will quickly undermine any chance of a respectful parental relationship on the part of the child.

This unhappily ending episode started off being about rowing. I fear it finished somewhere else entirely. I haven't coached for that school since. Touchline Dads can do real damage.

Round One

I don't even recall who it was we raced first. I know I could look it up, but really I couldn't be arsed. We were in no mood to dally around. We knew the starting drill by

Winning easily in one of the early rounds

now and were just determined to blast down the course and send a message to every other crew. We also badly needed to shake off and bury forever that dreadful loss to Durham.

I do recall however that once we got going, we were immediately ahead and moving further away with every stroke. The concentration was intense, and it was with some surprise that I noticed us passing the Barrier with no sign of the other crew.

'They've stopped' I called out, hoping we could take the rate down and just paddle home.

'Shut up,' Jarlath snarled at me, 'we're doing the full course.'

There wasn't a sound in the boat other than the rhythmic slam of the oars at the finish of each stroke. I went back to work. There was no distraction and I concentrated on the rhythm. Jarlath stayed completely quiet, which was partly why he was such a superb boat driver. If it didn't need saying, he wouldn't say it. He could sense when it was working, and right then and there it was working.

It made for an eerie experience. I wasn't conscious of anything anywhere except the preparation for the next stroke. Neatly out of the water, quick hands away from the body, slow to break the knees, and then control the movement up the slide. Except I didn't feel I had to think it all through. It just seemed to be there of its own accord. All I needed to do was keep everything moving in a controlled fashion.

The boat seemed to get faster and faster as we went down the course and the rowing seemed to get easier and easier regardless of how much power I put in. I seemed to be able to pour the power on to the oar without suffering any oxygen deprivation. The hairs on the back of my neck were up. We were flying, the boat seemed to be doing all the work, and it felt so comfortable. I don't know from where John magicked up that rhythm, but it felt like all his rowing prowess was now zeroing in on these last few days.

We went through the finish and still Jarlath didn't speak. As we rounded the corner heading for the landing slips he called 'wind down' and we slowed but moved directly to land. I remember hopping out of the boat feeling as if we had finished a light outing.

I heard Robin asking John, 'how was it?'

'Really good,' he said, 'fast, smooth and controlled.'

He was right. When the times were published that evening for all the races in the event, we were over 10 seconds faster than even the closest race.

But for all that, we knew how fickle Henley could be, and how things could quickly change. A fast crew, winning an early race comfortably, can relax as they paddle home and deliberately post a slower time. The wind can change during the day. The water flow can change between morning and afternoon and especially overnight. Most of all, virtually every crew gets faster and faster as they progress through the rounds, and shaving up to ten seconds off a previous time is by no means unknown.

Finally, the veteran rowing reporter David Fairs ambled up suggesting that one of the Stewards had confessed that our time was the result of a mistake. We didn't believe him, but he knew a potentially cocky crew when he saw one, and he knew cocky crews rarely won. We were amused but wary.

Supper that night was a quiet affair. Doc Terry had enquired about our time and for the first time since that initial breakfast you could see he was starting to wonder whether in fact it might actually be a decent crew that would mark his and Elaine's first foray into hosting. He was looking very thoughtful as we continued to impersonate a cloud of locusts descending on his dining table.

Second Round

The boys from Queen's University Belfast were next up but we had raced them earlier in Ireland and knew we wouldn't have a problem. They were in a rebuilding cycle and gaining experience, as we had done two years before. They were despatched in a similar time by a distance of three lengths, and we knew we had considerably more speed in the locker.

Already the Doc was starting to sense that his initial disbelief of John's response on the first morning had been way off the mark. He now went out towards the other limb and came to dinner that night armed with each of the times and winning distances for every other crew in the event. The coaches let him speak, but I could see the glances being exchanged between them as they realised that unknowingly he might raise the stress levels that they were so carefully managing. They had a quiet word afterwards, but even we could see the tension was building within him as he aligned himself completely with the crew.

The Quarterfinal

University College and Hospital had packed their crew with some hardened experienced Boat Race oars, but again we came home comfortably, albeit the time was a lot quicker than the previous day so maybe they pushed us along somewhat.

It was almost routine now for the boat to feel fast at every outing. I was reminded of the famous difference between the amateur and the professional. The former practices until he gets it right. The latter practices until he can't get it wrong. The boat was professional.

The Semi-Final

The loss to Durham in Nottingham had been a serious wake-up call. After the successes there in previous years, losing had come out of the blue. In parallel, having set such a fast time for the first race, we realised that we now had a target on our backs. Durham might turn out to be this year's problem.

Sitting at the start waiting for the familiar routine, I didn't feel the usual nerves, even though I knew that this was likely the real final for us. We had seen no one else capable of beating us apart from this crew.

Most of us knew that if we won this race, barring a severe accident, we would secure that oh-so-elusive target of the Ladies Plate for Trinity College Dublin on the following day. We also knew that it would probably end our rowing careers as other, less attractive, and arguably less professional but money making careers beckoned. None of us had any real family money behind us so we would have to work for a living. Rowing at that level required such a commitment that pursuing a working career in parallel would not have been an option.

There was therefore a coldness emanating from the crew as we settled into the boat and drew away from the launch slips heading for the start. I think we all realised that this race also marked the culmination of four years of dedication for many of us, and even more years for several of the crew. There was a real sense that what we could have had last year, but what was somehow beyond us, was not beyond us this year and we mustn't lose it.

Both crews started the race cleanly but as we passed the first marker our noses were in front. At the Barrier (two minutes or so out from the start), we were rowing to our potential and were further ahead. It didn't feel like we were struggling to maintain rate or power, and as we went up the course we were clearly leading but only by a length. Both crews were moving well and we knew we were not safe. The power in our boat was consistent; the run was good; there was no evidence of anyone losing concentration and rushing up the slide to the catch; but still we couldn't shake them.

It was then Jarlath simply said, 'remember Nottingham, *get away* from them!'

It was a brilliant call at a brilliant time, being halfway through the race. He knew we needed to kill off any hope they might have of mounting a dash at the finish. I think it was almost venom that I could feel coming into the boat as we all hardened on further. John took the rate up very slightly looking to match the power lift, and ever so gently we started moving away. It wasn't dramatic and it wasn't sudden, but it was consistent.

As every stroke came and went, we started to squeeze the life out of their race, and their hopes. And this typifies the requirement of being able to race at a serious level. During the race, at a time of maximum physical stress when the body is screaming for oxygen, when all the muscles are under the severest of strain, not only must the technique of handling the oar be maintained identically by each rower in the boat, but the thinking brain has to be decoupled from the pain-screaming physical body to maintain control, adjust a rate, even to decide to change nothing.

We came into the enclosures near the finish two lengths clear and, if anything, we were moving a little further away with every stroke. We went through the finish line and eased off the power but kept rowing. We were making the point that we could have done more.

There were no winning screeches or water slaps or even collapsing back on to the legs of the man behind. We kept moving. We had one hand on that old Ladies jug but still were taking nothing for granted.

Finally, the Final

We knew we should win it, but we had lost races in the past which we should have won. Personally, I was no longer worried about the race in the sense of the pain to come. I knew by now that I could deal with that. What was now concerning me greatly was that somehow we would goof it up, something would break, or some other black swan event would materialise out of nowhere.

We backed down onto the start gate and a pair of hands reached out from the chap lying prone to hold the boat in position. He grasped the stern as the opposition did the same. The umpire rose to his feet. Looking past him on his launch, I could see the drawn and nervous faces of Robin and the other handful of our supporters. The umpire rose and recited the now familiar instructions, and suddenly we were under way.

The start *was* a goof in some ways. We got away neatly enough but at the top of the island, being a few hundred metres out, we were down. The opposition had a small lead, and as they were on our right, I was facing them at the catch of every stroke. I could hear their cox screaming at them 'we have a man, now let's get two!' It was the first time in that entire regatta that someone led us. I think we were all concentrating so much on not doing something stupid that both the rate and power were probably a fraction less than we would have thrown at it had it been anything other than the final.

In other ways, it was not a goof. We had reasoned it out before the race that they would likely feel that their best chance to defeat us would be to try to unsettle us by blasting off as hard and as fast as they could, precisely in the hope that we would panic and wouldn't settle. It didn't work. We didn't panic and we did settle into our own rhythm. All of a sudden we were through them and had dropped them by half a length. At the Barrier we were moving away.

At that stage I recall it as being one of the quietest races I ever rowed, inside the boat 'bubble'. It was clearly down to the unbelievable concentration to ensure that we did everything perfectly and that we would not make the slightest error at any time in any way. Jarlath was again calmness personified. I vaguely remember a few 'keep it' and 'keep the concentration' calls spoken quietly through the microphone to the speakers under our seats as we came up the course. As we made the halfway point it was clear that only a disastrous accident now could cause us to lose. We had pulled right away.

We kept it unchanged as we went deeper into the race distance. There was a single and very brief familiar slamming sound as the eight oars exited the water simultaneously at the end of every stroke, and then silence as we slid forward gathering for the next entry point. The oars went in as one, levered through the water, and exited to the same slamming sound. It became mesmeric and almost the only sensation in the brain. One after another, repeated and repeated with mercifully no variation. The boat was running well, smooth and consistent, surging way from the residual puddles marking the eight oars' final positions for that stroke, and leaving six feet plus of distance before the eight oars slotted back into the water for the next one.

It was hard and controlled, but far from easy. A professional photograph was taken from water level as we passed into the enclosures and was circulated to us later. It showed every crew member grimacing and straining to get more oxygen as the levels declined with every successive stroke. We might have been comfortably ahead, but the opposition were a very fast crew (rather obviously as they also had made the final), and any mistake or the slightest letting up would undo us in a matter of seconds.

By now I suspect we were all dimly aware of the crowds starting to surround us as we came towards the long packed enclosure section of the course. Oddly, however, while out of the corner of my eye I could sense huge commotion on the riverbank, I heard little actual noise. The concentration level required within the boat was enormous. It was obviously vital to keep the timing at the catch of every stroke perfectly in tune with John, to the millimetre.

It was equally vital to keep the power on all the way through the stroke, and to ensure that the finish was strong and quick but neat. It was essential to avoid any emotional tearing at the oar. But most of all, we all had to keep the sense of the boat's rhythm to ensure that the work effort from all of us went through the stroke consistently at exactly the same time. And always the concentration.

We neared the last section of the course. I heard Jarlath asking John whether he wanted a final push. There was no doubt we had it in us. Rating in the low thirties, we could readily have managed more. But John was first and foremost a winner. However trite a phrase it is, it remains true that to finish first, first you have to finish. John knew, as by then we were all starting to recognise, that there was only one thing that could now stop us from winning. And that was us. He gave the order: 'no change'. No playing to the gallery. No flourishes. No nonsense. There was over a hundred years at stake.

We passed the Regatta Enclosure and came into the Stewards Enclosure arena. We passed the first and then the last grandstand. We passed the open area beyond them with the great 'results' oak tree. We passed the waterside seating area 50 yards from the end. Moments later, we flashed under the members' floating stand positioned by the finish post, and immediately crossed the line.

Winning painfully but comfortably

There was the usual water and back slapping and yelling within the boat but what I remember most vividly was the sudden arrival of a wall of noise directed at us. Rows and ranks of black and white blazers screaming at us from every side. A barrage of sound enveloping us. We had no idea so many people had arrived in support.

We pulled to the landing stage and clambered out, overrun by well-wishers. Everyone was indeed welcoming us, and being welcomed by us, but there were two men we wanted to see most. We knew the Big Mac was back in Dublin working, but we also knew Robin was slowly making his way from the umpire's boat across the boating lawn to us. He came to the slip and had eyes first for John. He knew what a difference he had made to the success of the crew. And then one by one he shook each

John in ecstasy, but I'm not sure which Lady is causing it. Either way it's Holy Grail time as, finally, a Trinity man gets to own The Ladies Plate (well for 5 minutes).

of our hands and clapped us on the back. A lifetime's ambition for him, vicariously achieved.

The Afters

There were various parties that night, and I suspect the makers of Pimm's had to revise upwards their expectation of that year's profits. I suppose I had my share, but I distinctly recall being stone cold sober all that evening. I met up with FG Jim who had travelled to see the race, and late that night we strolled down the riverbank.

'How does it feel?' he asked me.

'Relief,' I said, 'it's all I can feel.' That wasn't quite true. I was gripping the medal in my trouser pocket so hard it was making my wrist ache.

He immediately rationalised it out for me (the feeling, not the medal – that wasn't going anywhere). Without being overtly conscious of it, he said we had all carried the weight of three years' ambition and dedication on our shoulders.

The commitment to us from other people was enormous. Robin, Chris, Nick and Rob had given up so much of their time to coach us. The fellows who rowed in our squad knowing they were not in the final crew but provided competition and back up support also played a vital role. The financial support from the university and former Trinity men in our early days, Brian and Noel especially, was very substantial.

And finally our own families, wondering what on earth we were doing spending our lives mindlessly

Robin Tamplin (seated and pointing) enjoying a well earned drink after the final. The man standing with the neck collar is the late Gerry Blanchard. A former captain of the Boat Club, he suffered a dreadful car accident earlier that week. Despite a broken leg and severe neck injuries, he discharged himself from a London hospital and raced to Henley to see the Final.

paddling up and down a small twisty bit of river in Dublin when we should have been studying to become doctors, accountants, engineers, or famous vaccine inventors, but wholly supportive nonetheless. We could now feel for the first time that we had repaid those huge debts. As ever, Jim's analysis had hit the target.

Returns

There was a delightful outcome to follow back in Dublin. At a small victory dinner held sometime later in honour of the crew and coaches, Maurice Horan, who had captained Robin's losing crew in the 1950 final, quietly mentioned that he had been in recent correspondence with the captain of Leander Club, one of the rowing clubs based in Henley with an enviable history of rowing success.

It transpired that the night of their loss all those decades ago, one of Maurice's crew had 'liberated' the Leander flag from its habitual spot, fluttering above their boat club. Following our victory, Maurice wrote to the Leander captain, enclosing the perfectly preserved flag, and explaining that it had always been his intention to return it when Trinity next captured the Ladies Plate. Herewith.

The reply when it came was masterly. The captain thanked him for having returned the flag, mentioning gently that the club had wondered where it had got to all these years, and went on to wish Trinity every success at all future Henley Royal Regattas, not least because, 'who knows what else of our property you might return.' This exchange of letters was, for many years, displayed in a special cabinet in the Leander Club House, no doubt marking a welcome return of their missing standard.

There was another amusing outcome created in Ireland by a mischievous and clever sub-editor working for the *Independent* newspaper. While providing an accurate report on the outcome of the final, and the significance of the win, the headline on the Monday following the race read 'Trinity Ladies Win At Henley'. Technically, of course, the headline was quite correct. But it did cause friends of Jane's mother to telephone asking that she pass on their congratulations to her rowing daughter on a famous win. She did...

But There Was Some Confusion

We all knew in 1976 that we would meet Hartford in the semi-final. We could see they were fast and huge. We knew that they would have us for power, but could we get them through technique or fitness?

Personally, I spent the time before that race utterly dreading it. I knew it was going to be the complete opposite of the coxless IV races in that it was going to be hard and painful. And it was going to hurt the entire way down the course, but there was no way out. It had to be confronted.

In the 1977 campaign I had no such feelings of dread. I knew we would have to race hard, and I knew that Durham had beaten us just very recently, but I wasn't scared of them in the way that I was truly frightened by the looming Hartford confrontation. I could not get it out of my mind that my opposite number in the Hartford 6 seat weighed so much more than me. How on God's green earth could I pull harder than him? The race was going to kill me, but slowly, over six minutes. I couldn't of course pull harder than him and, as you now know, they did beat us.

The reality was that we had rowed that race as well as the crew were capable of doing so. We had been as fit as possible, possibly one of the fittest crews at the regatta thanks to the Robin/Chris plan having been closely followed. The stroke rate and racing tactics had been perfect throughout the race. All our power had been there throughout the race. The truth was that there was nothing more we could have done.

But I was bothered that I was not as upset by this as I always felt I should have been at that loss. Similarly, why was I not utterly overjoyed at winning the event in 1977?

A conversation years later with Robin went a long way to resolving this conundrum.

Sport is obviously about tests. Swifter, higher, stronger and so on. It might appear that sportsmen and women are testing themselves against someone else. Mostly, however, they are testing themselves against themselves.

My sporting test was in 1976. There were by then, and subsequently have been more hard races to be endured, but nothing has ever loomed over me as that awful 1976 semi-final. When it was over, however, I felt there was nothing more that I or our crew could have done.

I did not miss any training. I had not lightened up or eased back at any stage in any way throughout the previous years. I could not have run further, lifted more weights, or pulled more strokes. I could not have pulled harder for one single stoke. I also remain convinced that our boat had never gone as fast that year as it did during the Hartford race. There was simply nothing more that we were capable of doing. Sometimes, you run up against people who are simply swifter, higher or stronger on the day.

The reason I was not so upset, however, was because that was a test which I had passed in my own mind. I was testing myself and I knew I done everything I could and left nothing out there on the water during the race.

K.J. Mulcahy, E.M. O'Morchoe, D.J. Sanfey, J.P.D. Murnane, E.D.G. Weal

DUBC Progress in The
Trinity College, Dublin beat Selwyn College, Cambridge in 7.15 (not row'd out); Queen's Uni›
Durham University in 7.02 by 1¾ lengths; F

Senior VIII Other
Trinity at Home; Erne HoR; Dublin HoR; New Ross HoR; T
Nottinghamshire International Regatta.

The result of the race was maybe other people's test. Not mine.

In these circumstances it is not that there *is* no regret. It is that there *should* be no regret. We are not built to win everything at all times. Sometimes winning is just not possible.

Boat Club
gatta 1977
Challenge Plate

Hickey, R.I. Reilly, J.A. Macken, J.M.P. McGee, Coach: R.W.R. Tamplin

Challenge Plate 1977
fast in 7.17 by 3 lengths; University College and Hospital, London in 7.09 by 2½ lengths;
College, Cambridge in 6.53 by 3½ lengths

6/1977 Season
Cup; The University Championships; Athlone Regatta;
Day 1) and Senior A & Elite II (Day 2)

In 1977 I faced no such test. I didn't dread any of the races. I had no fear of test failure. It is true that I was worried about mucking it up somehow, or that someone else in the crew would muck it up, but it wasn't the same test. So with no test to overcome, there wasn't a huge feeling of achievement when the event finished.

I'm guessing that most Henley medals are in the winners' knicker and sock drawers. They don't tend to have pride of place on the family mantelpiece because those big chunks of metal are intrinsically meaningless. It's the personal test performance that matters.

Of course, it is very nice to win and I'm not saying that losing should ever be sweet and easy to swallow. But if you lose knowing that had you performed to your optimum you would have won, well then losing will be very sour.

Conversely, if you have done all you could to the best of your training and ability, well then the regret will be nowhere near as hard to take.

So that's why I wasn't totally shattered after losing to Hartford. Of course, I'd still rather have had the medal in 1976, but I have never felt since that it was deservedly my medal. I'm sure it sits properly in the (very big) sock drawer of my Hartford opposite number.

And maybe that's rowing in a nutshell. And maybe life too, in another nutshell. Life is full of tests. Maybe rowing teaches us how to deal with them as they arrive. Do the best we can, but if we fail in that despite everything, then we move on. Nothing more to be done this time round.

And the Answer Is?

Rowing is, and will hopefully always remain, an odd pastime. Fortunately, it can often be so boring for spectators that it has remained genuinely amateur, even if it is a long way these days from being amateurish. It is also an excellent sport for those who fear that they don't have fast hand-eye coordination and hence are not attracted to ball games. And, finally, it is also excellent in that it is perfectly suited to women just as much as it is to men.

As for me, I will always be grateful to Tom Noble and the others around for my direct involvement in the sport, and especially my introduction to DUBC. There is little doubt that it has shaped my life in so many positive ways.

What I was not expecting, however, was the satisfaction which can be derived from involvement in the sport without actually sitting in a boat. I was very conscious of how the Boat Club had in many ways made me, and so the year I left Trinity I did feel that I ought to give something back. I was also keen to see that the club would not drift immediately back into a form of mediocrity, having reached for such heights so recently.

I therefore volunteered to help, and ended up being the sole senior coach for the Boat Club for 1979/80, and shared the role with Dave Sanfey the following year. Genuinely, it was almost as satisfying as actually sitting in the boat. This did come as a surprise to me, and led me later to conclude that what I thought would be merely a dutiful task actually turned out to be a real pleasure.

Mind you, it was helped in the fact that crew I was coaching, which remained largely unchanged for those two years, was truly excellent. Perish the thought, but I have a feeling it might well have been faster than our 1977 bunch. It was an extraordinary crew also in terms of their commitment to the club and their individual successes in the multiplicity of careers they subsequently pursued. It did, however, suffer a staggering disappointment. In

Possibly one of the best rowing photos ever taken, this shows Yale about to beat Trinity by three feet in the semi-final of the Ladies Plate in 1979. The pain on virtually every oarsman's face is readily apparent. By this point in the race these men have raced neck and neck for over 2,000 metres, and despite their immense strength and fitness, they have run out of oxygen almost completely, and are truly desperate to suck in any air they can. The technique being maintained at this late stage is exemplary.

The man immediately in front of the Trinity cox, Gerry Macken, collapsed unconscious at the end. He is the brother of John Macken, who occupied the same position in the author's crew, and went on subsequently to win the Ladies Plate on a number of occasions with different crews. The man behind him, Karl Zinsmeister, had taken a year out from Yale to row for Trinity. In a terrible irony, his former friends and fellow oarsmen beat him by the narrowest of margins to take the trophy that year.

1980 the crew got to the semi-final of the Ladies Plate only to be beaten by Yale by a heart-breaking distance of three feet (see photo next page). After a race distance of precisely 2,112 metres, with the crews neck and neck the whole way, to lose by the smallest distance allowed was almost impossible to take. It is a tribute to their fortitude, however, that never once since that day did I ever hear any of them moaning about the outcome. More confirmation I guess that if you give your all and it doesn't quite work out, you don't feel quite so heartbroken.

And, of course, as you would expect of the heartbreak in the story of Trinity and the Ladies, Yale went on to take the trophy that year, winning the final comfortably. But that's the Ladies. It can be somewhat random and you just have to suffer it. I suppose it would be called character building, and maybe that's why rowing was invented.

Nothing more to say really, is there? Well, I suppose I could apologise for putting all this stuff down on paper, but someone had to do it...

APPENDIX

The table on the following page is extracted from the 1977 regatta programme and shows that the 1975 Trinity crew equalled the record to the first marker (the Barrier) in the first round.

Despite this achievement, the crew were beaten by MIT, but they had to break the record to the second marker (Fawley) to do so.

They in turn were beaten by the ultimate winners, University of London, who also had to break the Fawley record, and the course record, to take the trophy that first year of our campaign. (I'm trying to explain here that we were fast. Even though we lost.)

The table also shows that in 1976 Trinity College, Hartford had to take a full six seconds off the record to defeat us that year. They beat us by a length. Which means we beat the record by three seconds.

So again we were fast, even faster than before. And still, again we lost. Until 1977 came along…

THE FASTEST RECORDED TIMES

Official times to Fawley were instituted in 1906, and to Remenham Barrier in 1929.

These Tables commence with the Records as they stood prior to 1975.

§   *denotes times recorded in heats.*

Where the same crew achieved the same time more than once in the same regatta it is not repeated.

Heat times shown on the same line were not necessarily achieved on the same day.

GRAND	Barrier	Fawley	Finish
Ratzeburg R.C., Germany, 1965	1.46	3.00	6.16
Harvard University, U.S.A., 1975			6.13§
Leander & Thames Tradesmen's R.C. 1975			6.13§
LADIES'			
D.S.R.Laga, Holland, 1973	1.52§		
Harvard University, U.S.A., 1973	1.52§	3.09§	
Univ. of Washington, U.S.A., 1973	1.52§		
Univ. of Wisconsin, U.S.A., 1973			6.32§
University of London, 1975	1.52§		
Trinity College, Dublin, Eire, 1975	1.52§		
Durham University, 1975	1.51§		
Isis B.C., 1975	1.48§	3.09§	
M.I.T., U.S.A., 1975		3.09§	
University of London, 1975		3.08§	6.30§
University of London, 1975		3.06	
Trinity Coll., Hartford, U.S.A., 1976			6.24§
THAMES			
Leander Club, 1968	1.51§		
Princeton University, U.S.A., 1973		3.08§	6.33§
Quintin B.C., 1973	1.51§	3.08§	
Univ. of Wisconsin, U.S.A., 1973			6.33§
Quintin B.C., 1975	1.51§		
Christiania Roklub, Norway 1975	1.51§		
Garda Siochana, Eire, 1975	1.50§		
Quintin B.C., 1975	1.50§	3.07§	
Leander Club, 1975	1.50§		
Christiania Roklub, Norway 1975..	1.50§		
Quintin B.C., 1975		3.06§	
Quintin B.C., 1975	1.49§	3.05§	
Henley R.C., 1976			6.32§
Christiania Roklub, Norway 1976..	1.49§	3.04§	6.25§
PRINCESS ELIZABETH			
Ridley College, Canada, 1973	1.53§	3.11§	6.38§
St. Paul's, Concord, U.S.A., 1975	1.52§	3.11§	6.36§
Ridley College, Canada, 1975		3.11§	
Ridley College, Canada, 1975	1.52§	3.10§	6.35§
Ridley College, Canada, 1975			6.32

AFTERWORD:
THE RETURN TO HENLEY

In 2017 we were very fortunate to be able to return to the Henley Royal Regatta to celebrate our famous victory 40 years earlier. What follows is a photographic account of that lovely event.

Kieran, the author, Ted and John looking amused before taking to the water for a 40 year winner's anniversary row past.

The boat used in the 2017 winner's row past, named in honour of our late coach.

The Hickey family at Henley. The author and Alexander bookending daughters and best friends Jess and Sally, with the ever patient Jane holding it all together. All are triathletes and/or rowers with decent pedigrees, save for the author. He's still trying, in every sense, as the family constantly tells him.

The 1977 crew rowing towards the finish line at the end of the 2017 row past. A slight weight differential in the crew may have appeared over those 40 years ....

Back on the water ... forty years later.

The 1977 crew after receiving their medals and trophy.

Sartorial splendour at Henley ...

*Rory, John, the author, Kieran and Ted all wearing their anniversary caps.
Dave Sanfey getting sartorial revenge for the author's failure to dress properly
in the winning Nottingham photo two years previously. Dave Weale in
sunglasses hiding from his bookie no doubt, and James smiling his watchful
smile at the rear. Seated in front is Brian Persson, the coach who enthused
so many of the 1973 maidens to stick at rowing and hence, knowingly or
unknowingly, was another foundation stone of the win.*

*And to cap it all, Kieran, John, the author and Ted subtly
reminding everyone when* they *won.*

*Dr. Terry and Elaine Dudeney, our house hosts in 1977,
motoring up to watch the 2017 row past.*

The author and John sharing a laugh.

Robin who sadly died before the reunion took place.

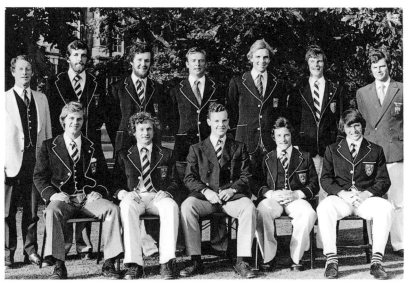

The formal winning crew photo taken in Front Square of Trinity.
The man on the extreme right is Bruce Carter, a former British
Olympic rower and occasional coach to the crew, and the chap
seated in the centre is George De Courcy Wheeler, the Boat Club
captain in 1977, though not in the crew that year.

243